Critical Acclaim for the Work of R. Eric Gustafson

"This intriguing modern-day *Odyssey* about a creative, outrageous, and charming knight errant searching for life's meaning takes an extraordinary turn. *Cinderella Is A Man* is a witty, titillating, extremely well-written story with an inspiring, heart-warming denouement."
 —Ruth Warrick, actress

"If life is an opera, then Eric Gustafson hits all the high notes. He designs the sets and costumes, too, and assembles an all-star cast from across the panorama of modern life. He's offering readers one of the best seats in the house. A fascinating memoir by a fascinating man."
 —Michael Redmond, music critic

"In his enchanted kingdom, Eric Gustafson once presented concerts, lectures, exhibitions, and theatricals in intimate, lovely settings imbue with a flavor that is uniquely his. Compassionate, original, vibrant, spontaneous, unpredictable, this flavor carried over to the dinners, balls, fêtes that made Eric's world as close as one gets these days to the court of his mentor, Louis XIV. To the large and adoring circle who has surrounded him, his ability to tend to what he would call "the Garden of Life" made Eric's presence a vivid and compelling example of a life of art, which is of course the Art of Living. He swaggered through several careers: New York art and antiques specialist, gallery director, curator of theater designs and museum exhibitions; and, he achieved a unique apotheosis as a Renaissance impresario in New Jersey's posh central hills as founding director of Apollo Muses Center for the Arts. Author, travel journalist, and lecturer presented him with more hats to don. His *bon vivant* lifestyle of rubbing elbows

with celebrities fueled the peripatetic quest for self-fulfillment. His on-going quest was to connect his life to his dreams. We all share this yearning, and Eric's experience was a quavering candle in a speeding world that has all too little time or energy for dreams."
   —Bruce Whitacre, Executive Director of Theatre Forward

"A lifetime's uncompromising devotion to the arts, threaded with personal insecurity, excess, rehab. And finally, acceptance of a kindly divaship. Courageous and inspiring."
   —Valmai Howe Elkins, author of *The Dreams of Zoo Animals*

"I admire all that you've done to promote art and artists. They are noble efforts and you should be proud of your accomplishments."
   —Frederica von Stade, international opera star

"'Knew everyone, went everywhere, and did everything' might well describe the journey of Bronx-born *bon vivant* Eric Gustafson. This is likely to be the most intimate peek into the glitz, glamour, and glory — and the perils and pitfalls — of high culture, art, and entertainment you've ever read. George Bernard Shaw said he wanted to die all used up. Gustafson is on track to do exactly that, for he has held nothing back."
   —Larry Dossey, MD, author of *One Mind*

"Thanks for your goodwill. friendship, and kind support. I love your personality, wit, and social genius. My best to you always."
   —Cyrus Casells, poet

"*Cinderella Is A Man* is a very personal confirmation of the regenerative power of the arts."
   —Celeste Holm, Academy Award–winning actress

"Eric Gustafson's remarkable journey from the streets of the Bronx to the elegant haunts of the glittering and famous, an odyssey of self-image molded by the movies, theater, ballet, and opera, is also a cautionary tale of giddy, alcohol-fueled excess, dawning self-awareness and redemption. His tale is both deliciously gossipy and spiritually enlightening. And what more could you ask?"

    —Jonathan Richards, actor, cartoonist, movie critic,
       co-author of *Nick and Jake*

"The truly amazing testament to luck, pluck, and greatly-deserved rewards. The pinpoint recall of pin-pricked illusions—unsentimental, smart as a whip—and happily, as well and rightly mastered from the performances of his avowed role model, Mae West, the whip is turned not on self, but on the big cats in the gilded cage. Eric has come through-come out of the cage very much more alive than ever. The big cats can go back to sleep-their roaring is of small interest to us now: we want to see what Eric is going to do next. Bravo!"

    — Jimmy McCourt, author *Mawrdew Czgowchwz*

Also by Eric Gustafson

The Court Theaters of Europe, 1982
Cinderella Is a Man: A Picaresque Passage to Serenity, 1998
India: Paradox & Treasures, Vol. 1 2004
India: Paradox & Treasures, Vol. 2, 2005
Ganesha & Friends: Images of India, 2007
Expect the Unexpected: Adventures of a Westerner Sitting in the Lap of Mother India, 2009
Last Guy Waltzing: A Tale of Reinvention, 2013
My Beloved Southwest: A Scrapbook Reflecting Memories of People and Places in the Land of Enchantment, 2017
A Kaleidoscope: Fragments of Memory, 2020

A Path Lit by Stars

A Path Lit by Stars:

Reminiscences

by

R. Eric Gustafson

with a prologue by

Jonathan Richards and Claudia Jessup

A Path Lit by Stars: Reminiscences.
Copyright © 2025 R. Eric Gustafson

Cover and book design by Jordan Jones

Cover image: "Path To The Stars" Michael Shainblum/Stocksy - stock.adobe.com. Used by permission.

Author photograph, courtesy of R. Eric Gustafson.

Photographic credits for additional images begin on page 172.

All rights reserved. No part of this publication may be reproduced, stored in a retrieval system, or transmitted in any form or by any means, electronic, mechanical, photocopying, recording or otherwise without the prior permission of the publisher.

Library of Congress Control Number: 2026930239

ISBN   Paper   978-1-58775-062-5
              E-Book 978-1-58775-063-2

1 3 5 7 9 10 8 6 4 2

Coyote Arts LLC
PO Box 6690
Albuquerque, New Mexico 87197-6690
coyote-arts.com

Dedication

*The Venerable Robina Courtin
together with Frank Hoffman and Peter Stephenson,
whose guidance and encouragement were invaluable.*

Acknowledgment

*Jordan Jones and Leslie Stahlhut at Coyote Arts
for their efforts and talents in the production of this volume.*

Contents

Finding the Path by Jonathan Richards and Claudia Jessup	3
The Constellation	9
Peter O'Toole / Judy Garland	11
Joan Crawford	13
Christina Crawford	15
Aaron Copland	17
Risë Stevens	19
Christine Jorgensen	21
Josephine Baker	23
James Dean	25
Georgia O'Keeffe	27
Ruth Warrick	29
Celeste Holm	31
Salvador Dalí	33
Lotte Lenya	35
Rudolf Nureyev / Eric Bruhn	37
Rita Hayworth	39
Groucho Marx	41
Veronica Lake	43
Tallulah Bankhead	45
Jackie Kennedy	47
Harry S Truman	49
Lee Radziwill	51
Doris Duke	53

Grace Bumbry	54
Sir Harold Acton	57
Queen Helen	59
Dame Joan Sutherland	61
Beverly Sills	63
Andy Warhol	64
Alvin Ailey	67
Greta Garbo	69
Anthony Perkins	70
Edward Mulhare / Jennie Tourel	73
Leonard Bernstein	74
Virgil Thompson	77
Zsa Zsa Gabor	79
Robert Indiana	81
Dennis Hopper	83
Frederica von Stade	85
Wyatt Cooper / Gloria Vanderbilt	87
Samuel Barber	89
Gian Carlo Menotti	90
King Gustav III / Queen Sylvia	93
Willem de Kooning	95
Gayelord Hauser	97
Elizabeth Taylor	99
R. C. Gorman	100
Betty Ford	103
Catherine Deneuve	105
Holly Woodlawn	107
The Duke of Devonshire	109
John XXIII	111
Lillian Gish	113
Greer Garson	115
James Baldwin	117
Leslie Caron	119
Jean-Louis Barrault	121

Jane Goodall	123
Alexandra Danilova	125
Tennessee Williams	127
Mae West	128
William Hurt	130
Martha Mitchell / Truman Capote	132
Edward Albee	135
Ray Bradbury	137
Madeleine Albright	139
Leontyne Price	141
Ethel Merman	143
Princess Margaret / Antony Armstrong-Jones	145
Kitty Carlisle Hart	147
Cliff Robertson / Dina Merrill	149
Rock Hudson	151
Libby Holman	153
Van Johnson	155
Hermione Gingold	157
Robert Stack / Janet Leigh	158
Jerome Hines / Franco Corelli	160
Oliver Smith	163
Cecil Beaton	165
Anne Jackson / Eli Wallach	167
Clare Boothe Luce	168
Epilogue	170
Photographic Credits	172
About the Author	183

Finding the Path

by Jonathan Richards and Claudia Jessup

The house sat on a tree-shaded lot in the northeast corner of the Bronx. The house is still there, but the lot is gone. Today it's squeezed shoulder-to-shoulder between soulless concrete commercial buildings.

In the Thirties and Forties, when young Eric Gustafson was growing up in that New York borough, his home was a bucolic haven where he and his sister played and planted flowers around the delightful playhouse their father's workmen had built for them. But after a while, things began to turn sour. Eric's father, a genial Swede who had jumped ship and established himself in the construction business in New York, was a glad-handing extrovert who enjoyed a few drinks with the boys. His mother remained a shy Swedish peasant woman who never quite adapted to the new world. She baked incessantly to battle her sense of displacement, giving away so many cookies and cakes to acquaintances and church functions that her children started calling her "Mrs. Santa Claus." And like Santa, she grew very plump. She resented her husband's easy assimilation, and her discontent grew apace with his drinking. Soon the fights became a regular part of the domestic scene, and the house that Eric called home began to lose its appeal.

Around 1950, Eric's father built the family a new brick house facing Pelham Bay Park, but they soon removed to a country place, a Victorian house in Montrose in the Hudson Valley. Still in school, Eric was left behind on his own in the Bronx house for long stretches, under the theoretical care of his older brother, a college boy who seldom bothered to come home. Eric battled his intense loneliness by listening to classical music and opera, and taking long walks in the park across the way.

More and more, the boy began to seek refuge at the movies. In the movies people were refined, they were elegant, they were beautiful. They spoke with clear and lovely diction, they danced divinely, they loved romantically. Stars like Orson Welles and Rita Hayworth, William Powell and Myrna Loy, Olivia de Havilland and Errol Flynn felt more like family and friends than the real thing. With the Bronx coming to seem like an alien planet on which he had been inexplicably marooned, Eric came home to the movies.

When he was accepted at the prestigious Stuyvesant High School on East 15th Street in Manhattan, that gulf grew wider. He studied speech and theater, and left the rough accents of his native Bronx behind. His way home from school passed through the Elysian Fields of the old Metropolitan Opera House on 39th Street, where a two-dollar standing room ticket opened the door to voices like Maria Callas, Robert Merrill, and Leontyne Price. Just beyond the opera lay the star-studded Great White Way where the Golden Age of Broadway offered Brando and Tennessee Williams and The King and I through those magical years. With temptations like those strewn in his path, it was an easy matter to take the boy out of the Bronx, and the Bronx out of the boy.

A happy gift of natural beauty didn't hurt. Young Eric, as he grew into manhood, was blessed with the face of an angel, the cheekbones of a Viking, and the torso of a Greek statue. From his apprenticeship at the movies, he learned to dress with flair and style. He spoke with elegance and wit, he developed (in Noel Coward's phrase) "a talent to amuse." He watched, and he listened.

Returning from a trip to Europe with his lover David Wallace (nephew of Bess Truman) in 1959, he was determined to live on the posh Upper East Side of Manhattan, and to find employment nearby so he would not have to stoop to the indignities of public transportation. He walked into the famed Parke-Bernet Galleries, the glamorous Manhattan art auction house on Madison Ave whose clientele included socialites and wannabes with deep pockets, decorators, collectors, and museum curators. He asked for a job and was hired on the spot. Eric absorbed culture like a sponge. He developed a keen eye for human nature and the fancies and foibles of the rich and famous.

One day Greta Garbo came into the gallery. The reclusive star, conspicuous in white bobby-socks and sneakers and a plastic raincoat and hat, spotted the young employee across the room. "Who is that beautiful young man?" she asked in her distinctive murmur. They were introduced. "Gustafsson," she said. "My name was Gustafsson before I changed it. You could be my nephew." From then on, she was Aunt Greta.

Stars who crossed Eric's path in those early days included Tallulah Bankhead, Celeste Holm, Rudolf Nureyev, and a youthful Leonard Bernstein just returned to a hero's New York welcome from a triumphant visit to the Soviet Union. Ruth Warwick, the actress who had played Kane's first wife in Orson Welles's *Citizen Kane* (and would later gain even greater fame as the imperious Phoebe Tyler for many years on the TV soap *All My Children*), was a mentor whom Eric credits with teaching him how to have self-confidence in being around celebrities.

The French have a term, *enfilade*, that refers to the graceful arrangement of doors in a chateau, lined up to facilitate easy movement from one room to the next in a well-planned flow. Eric's life has been a kind of *enfilade*, with doors opening onto new rooms as old ones close behind him. As he sees it, this is a matter of design, not accident — setting one's life on a certain course produces results that may not always be predictable, but they follow a pattern. Not all the rooms of his life's passage have been orderly, not all have been happy, not all have been well-defined. But as his own karmic *enfilade* unfolded, a new door has always managed to swing open at the right moment; and Eric was ready to walk through.

The many friendships he has made along the way have been sustaining, exciting, rewarding, and defining. A lot of the most important have been with women. Surprisingly, this list even includes a wife. In the middle of the last century, when Eric Gustafson was coming of age, homosexuality was held in a very different regard than it is today, subject to penalties both social and legal, and there was a period when he wasn't sure which way to jump. He had a dear, close friend in those days, a lovely girl named Lucia. They went to foreign films, they dined at quaint restaurants, they had fun together. It wasn't too much of a stretch to think that that sort of friendship might be supposed to lead into marriage. And so they got married.

It didn't take long for Eric to realize that he had jumped the wrong way. The marriage lasted about a year, ended amicably, and Eric moved on. There were no more marriages, but there were deep platonic relationships with women, a few achieving what Eric considers soul mate status, and none more so than Nina Micheleit. He met her in Provincetown in the late Fifties, where Nina managed her brother-in-law's art gallery, and Eric worked during the summer as a waiter, a model, and a handyman. Their friendship was deep and profound.

And there was Ysabel Aya, a relationship that spanned continents and decades. It was Ysabel, Eric recalls, who taught him to drink in the morning without guilt. Waking after a drunken night of partying, when he had crashed at her Manhattan apartment, Ysabel would say "Pick up the phone, darling, and tell the maid to bring some vodka." If he demurred, she replied "Don't be ridiculous, darling, it gets you on your feet!"

Another friendship that lasted decades followed with Lila Luce Tyng, the first wife of publishing magnate Henry Luce. Lila was like a big sister with whom Eric traveled and entertained, and on whose New Jersey Lu Shan Farm estate he created and ran his famed Apollo Muses Center for the Arts for a quarter of a century.

Along the way, there was a vast rogue's gallery of celebrities. Some became friends, some lovers, some were encountered like ships crashing in the night. They included an ex-president, Harry Truman, who managed to steer Eric away for a stiff drink or two in the privacy of his study, secluded from the disapproving gaze of the prim Mrs. Truman, whom Eric dubbed "Baptist Bess". There was another president's wife, Jaqueline Kennedy, who cruised him with such a frank stare that he felt he was being stripped naked on the street. The roster included film stars, some of the very same ones who had molded his outlook on life as a kid growing up at the movies. Others came from the worlds of music and art, ballet and opera, fashion and drama and literature, politics and the society pages.

Dealing with all this heady company required extra support to fortify the shy boy from the Bronx, and that support arrived in the form of alcohol. Booze was a steadying friend to lean on, it provided courage, ease, and confidence. It got out of hand. It became a monster that threatened to destroy him.

And then another door opened.

"Get your ass over to Betty Ford." The words were addressed by Elizabeth Taylor to the artist R. C. Gorman in Taos, New Mexico, but Eric was there, and he understood that those words applied just as directly to him. He took her admonition to heart, and picked up the phone that same day and got his ass over to Betty Ford. He credits Taylor with saving his life, and setting him on the path of sobriety that has endured for forty years.

Another door opened, and this one led to India. Although Eric has had intimate affairs with many famous men, and plenty of flings with men unknown to the gossip pages as well, he has never had a relationship that lasted long enough to be considered a life partnership, or a soul mate. He came as close to that as he would ever come with Raja, a young Brahmin whom he met on a trip to the subcontinent at the millennium. He fell in love with India, and he fell in love with Raja. The relationship lasted a decade, but ultimately the complexities of the two countries, and the distances, and the cultural chasm, along with the gap in their ages, led Eric to reluctantly cut the relationship loose.

There have been other doors, other adventures, other passions, and one of the most enduring of this last period of his life has been his discovery of and immersion in Buddhism, which he practices at his home of the past few decades in Santa Fe, New Mexico. These days his life is quiet, surrounded by friends and his closest companion, his beloved cockerpoo Cyrus.

A journey that began in the Bronx as a lonely kid with a vivid internal life has come full circle, after the decades of stars, sex, and glamorous living, to an internal spirituality and a Buddhist guiding light of inner peace. His life is a distant echo of those riotous years when the world was his playground, the arts were his palette, and his path was lit by a galaxy of stars.

And now, a few words about those stars ....

The Constellation

Some of this I have written about, but taken as a whole it makes a staggering array to light up any life. What was it that precipitated all these meetings with the very rich and famous? Yes, I was in love with celebrity and put myself in the path of many of them. Often, they initiated the meetings. Was it my youthful good looks paired with a whiff of innocence? My appearance, well-dressed and groomed, with a talent for dancing? My energetic lifestyle, lived with a touch of elegance? Being well educated and versed in the arts was a bonus. Or perhaps it was that they sensed that I cared about them.

The cast of characters:

1. Peter O'Toole in Lawrence of Arabia (1962)

2. Judy Garland in a publicity still from The Harvey Girls (1946)

Peter O'Toole
Actor

Judy Garland
Actress, singer, dancer

I was working public relations at the premiere of Richard Brooks' film of *Lord Jim*, which opened in New York City in the winter of 1965. A supper dance at the Astor Hotel on Times Square was held following the New York premiere. There, the movie's Irish star, Peter O'Toole, approached me and asked me if I would introduce him to Judy Garland. O'Toole had been imbibing heavily, but then so had I. Neither of us, however, were as far into our cups as La Garland, whom we found slumped over her dinner plate. With a little effort we roused her and got her on her feet, I made the introductions, and a photographer snapped a photo of the two stars. I may have been the only one of us who had any recollection of it the next day. O'Toole thanked me and shook my hand. It was like squeezing a damp sponge. It was oddly unappealing in such a gorgeous man. What a pity! During the course of the evening, O'Toole engaged in some inappropriate behavior in the men's room which MGM paid a good deal of money to hush up.

3. Joan Crawford, 1948

JOAN CRAWFORD
Actress

Crowds had gathered outside Loew's State Theater in Times Square for the premiere of *Lord Jim*. A roped-off space for those alighting from limousines was secured and maintained by uniformed guards. I stood nearby to alert the press to the famous personages arriving. A stretch limo pulled up, provocatively stopping about ten feet out from the curb. No door opened. Finally a face appeared at the window. A wave. Joan Crawford! As soon as people realized who it was, excitement spread. Slowly the door opened. A high-heeled slipper appeared. A leg. The actress stepped out, in slow motion. She stood, allowing her bugle-beaded ensemble to drape gracefully as she gave another wave, and then began to walk slowly toward the curb. By now the crowd was feverish with excitement. Crawford looked toward the theater entrance and waved again, seeming to recognize someone she knew. It was the epitome of theatricality. I learned a lot about diva-hood from this encounter.

It was especially striking as it stood in contrast to our meeting a few evenings earlier. I was in a Fifth Avenue penthouse room waiting for a gathering of board members to discuss last-minute details for the gala premiere. A woman in a simple dress arrived, and walked over to a bar that had been set up for the occasion. "Hello, John," she greeted a popular TV host who was standing at the bar. When I heard that famous voice I realized that it was Joan Crawford, and I had not recognized her. Stars have the ability to radiate or not, depending on the circumstances. It must be a relief not to have to be "on" all the time!

4. Christina Crawford in a promotional photograph, 1961

Christina Crawford
Actress, writer

Joan Crawford's adopted daughter Christina lived in a simple ground floor apartment in an Upper East Side brownstone. On the occasions when I visited her, her mother's aura was always present. My strongest recollection of her is of a very affable Tina sitting cross-legged on her mattress, in front of a huge headshot of her mother that leaned against the back wall. I believe Tina liked to think she was reflecting her mother by using that photo as a backdrop while she adopted a similar facial expression. It seemed to supply her with an identity that she craved, despite the negative feelings that she'd later express in her book *Mommie Dearest.*

Her brother Christopher, also adopted, seemed a much more tormented soul. I met him while visiting friends who worked in the display department of Bloomingdale's, where Chris also had a job. He had a pockmarked face and a drab personality. I imagine he had been suffocated by his adoptive mother.

R. Eric Gustafson

5. *Aaron Copland, 1962*

Aaron Copland
Composer, musician, conductor, critic

Aaron Copland came to Stuyvesant High School in lower Manhattan during the late Forties to talk to us teenagers about the importance of classical music in our lives. This brilliant composer and mentor to other musicians was a tireless proponent of American music. His enthusiasm resonated with me and encouraged me to expand my exposure to classical music. He triggered in me a powerful love for music that has carried through my life.

6. Risë Stevens, 1959

Risë Stevens
Operatic mezzo-soprano

"Sincerely Yours". That's how the great opera star Risë Stevens signed her responses to my fan mail. It was also the title of her 1949 four-disc 78 rpm album on the Columbia label, one of my treasured possessions. As a young teenager I bought two-dollar standing room tickets at the old Metropolitan Opera House to take in her performance as Carmen, her signature role in the Forties and Fifties. She made frequent appearances on the Bell Telephone Hour and other TV programs, and I would write in for tickets, and afterward go backstage to have her sign my album or a publicity photo. Her saucy Carmen in Seville offered a vivacious counterpoint to my life as a Lutheran boy living in the Bronx (where she too had been born to Scandinavian parentage a couple of decades before me). As I grew older, I was drawn ever more deeply into the magical world of operatic music, and fell in love with other operas and divas. However, Stevens' *Carmen* always remained a high point in my early opera-going experiences, and cast a sensual spell over my expanding youthful imagination.

7. *Christine Jorgensen with Eric Gustafson, at the Scandinavian Societies of New York Woman of the Year Award Ceremony, 1953*

CHRISTINE JORGENSEN
Transgender pioneer, actress, singer

On March 7th, 1953, the year after her ground-breaking gender transformation in Denmark, Christine Jorgensen received the Woman of the Year Award from the Scandinavian Societies of New York. I was there. Along with members of my Swedish Messiah Lutheran Church, the Swedish Folk Dance group to which I belonged, and some college friends, this astonished but fascinated 17-year-old attended the ceremony in the Manhattan Center hotel ballroom. In the group picture that was taken, I can be seen at the left shoulder of this phenomenon. Christine Jorgensen's was the first widely publicized sex change procedure, and it stunned the world. I marveled at how beautiful she was at this public appearance. In 1975 I saw her again when I attended Johnny Carson's 50th birthday party at Toots Shor's, a legendary New York watering hole. I was seated at a table with several glamorous actresses including Arlene Dahl and Ruth Warrick, having a merry time, when I noticed Christine sitting alone across the room. She had a martini in front of her and a cigarette in her hand, and she looked dejected and old. It made a sad contrast to the glamorous creature I remembered from a distant time.

8. Josephine Baker, circa 1927

JOSEPHINE BAKER
Dancer, singer

Josephine Baker celebrated her birthday with a fundraiser for needy children at a small, elegant New York City disco that was closed for this special event. She was wearing a peek-a-boo black gown that I felt was inappropriate to her age. I was waltzing with my friend Alice Fordyce, sister of the famous philanthropist Mary Lasker (whose invitation we had used to get in). I became aware of Miss Baker observing us from the edge of the dance floor. Afterward she came over to compliment me on my skillful dancing. Coming from this internationally famous performer, it was quite an honor.

9. James Dean, 1955

JAMES DEAN
Actor

"Was that who I think it was?" I asked my friend Terry, a fellow summer student at UCLA, as we left the restaurant. We had arrived for lunch at a crowded Hollywood Boulevard catery, and had made our way through the room searching for a place to sit. In the rear, at a large table, a young man sat alone. "Do you mind if we join you?" I asked. He gestured an invitation, and as we sat I got a closer look at him. It was James Dean! I was sure of it! At this point in his meteoric and tragically short career he had already made *East of Eden* and *Rebel Without a Cause,* and was at work on his final film, *Giant.* There was no mistaking that handsome face, but Terry and I respected his privacy, and only exchanged a few words with him as we sturdily tried to pretend that this screen idol was an ordinary diner like ourselves. Our constraint was amazing — as was he!

R. Eric Gustafson

10. Georgia O'Keeffe in Abiquiu, New Mexico, 1950

Georgia O'Keeffe
Artist

I had never met Georgia O'Keeffe, although we had some awareness of each other (I of her far more than she of me) by way of the Santa Fe art scene. So I was nonplussed when I saw her cutting her way toward me through the enormous crowd in the lobby of the Whitney Museum like a ship parting the waves, ignoring greetings from the hundreds who wanted to congratulate her on her retrospective opening that day. She walked up to me and extended her hand. "You are my friend," she said. It was astonishing.

11. Left to right: Celeste Holm, Eric Gustafson, and Ruth Warrick

Ruth Warrick
Actress

"You were my favorite movie star when I was a kid," I stammered nervously as I partnered Ruth Warrick around the First Class dance floor of the luxurious *Île de France*. My passage was below decks, but when I spotted her name on the famous ship's guest list, I donned my tuxedo on the second night out and sneaked up into First Class. I remembered Miss Warrick well from my youthful saturation in the movies. She had played the first wife of Charles Foster Kane in the Orson Welles classic *Citizen Kane*, and she would soon go on to enduring fame for many years as Phoebe Tyler Wallingford on the TV soap opera *All My Children*.

Little did I know when I booked passage in 1957 from Southampton to New York aboard the legendary ship that this would be a "ghost voyage", with only a small number of passengers. The *Île de France* had been laid up for repairs which were completed ahead of schedule, and she was making a hastily arranged trip to New York to pick up bookings there. The paucity of passengers made the crew anxious to please, and champagne flowed for what seemed like a merry private party.

I approached Ruth's table and asked her to dance. She graciously accepted, and thus began what was to become a long friendship spanning many decades. I was her escort to many glamorous events, and she was a fixture at my Apollo Muses Center of the Arts presentations. Ruth encouraged my self-confidence, and she shared with me many insights into the world of celebrity.

12. Celeste Holm with Eric Gustafson

Celeste Holm
Actress

Another regular visitor at my Apollo Muses events was Academy Award winner Celeste Holm (Best Supporting Actress, *Gentleman's Agreement* [1947]). She and her husband, the actor Wesley Addy, were always delighted at the diversity and quality of these Sunday afternoon offerings. On occasion they would come to dine in my garden at my home in Peapack, New Jersey. They lived a dozen miles away on Schooley's Mountain, when not at their duplex on Central Park West in New York City.

Celeste would tell wonderful stories about her career, such as her first big audition, for the role of Ado Annie in the original Broadway production of *Oklahoma,* when she was so nervous that she spilled her sheet music and had to scramble all over the stage picking it up. She sang a folk song for her audition number, and ended with a hog call. And the first rehearsal for the film *All About Eve,* when she arrived with a cheery "Good morning!" and Bette Davis growled "Oh God, it's going to be another of *those* productions." Some of her stories bordered on the risqué, which seemed to amuse her.

Wesley Addy died in 1996, and eight years later, on her 87th birthday, Celeste married a young operatic bass-baritone who was less than half her age. The family lawsuits that followed to break her irrevocable trust were prolonged and terribly costly, and left her in precarious financial condition by the time of her death. But years earlier, Celeste had confided in me that she did not intend to leave her children anything, saying they could fend for themselves.

13. Salvador Dalí and his wife Gala with friends, including, far right, Ysabel Aya, Eric Gustafson's "Colombian soul mate"

Salvador Dalí
Artist

The famed Surrealist surfed many of the same upscale New York events that I did. We acknowledged each other with social pleasantries, but nothing more, as I was not what he was looking for. Sometimes his wife Gala would join him, but only when he paid her to do so. How much she charged for these appearances depended on her interest in the event.

14. Lotte Lenya in The Threepenny Opera (1931)

LOTTE LENYA
Actress, singer

"I'm from Missouri, show me!" Lotte Lenya dared me. I rose to the challenge, mimicking her famous murderous kick as the Soviet villain Rosa Klebb in the James Bond film *From Russia with Love.* But unlike in the film, no dagger protruded from my shoe, and no damage was done other than our killing ourselves with laughter. We would meet occasionally at parties, and it always excited me. Lenya was a living legend. Twice married to the composer Kurt Weill, she had been a star since her breakthrough role as Jennie when his *The Threepenny Opera* opened in Berlin in 1928. She embodied a segment of twentieth century history from pre-Hitler Germany through her later career in post-WWII America in film, theater, and recordings. I felt enlivened and enriched in her company.

15. Rudolf Nureyev

16. Eric Bruhn

Rudolf Nureyev
Ballet dancer

"Sit up with the driver," I directed the great dancer, giving a firm shove to the brown corduroy trousers covering his taut ass as he started to back into the cab. Rudy gave me a startled look, but he complied. I wanted the back seat alone with my beloved Prince of Dance Eric Bruhn for a bit of intimate conversation. A little ego bruising was good for Rudy's dynamic personality, and Eric was amused. Rudy and I were to cross paths again a few times after Eric returned to Europe. The last time I saw him was on the stage of La Scala in Milan following one of his performances. I waited to be last in line to congratulate him so that we would not be interrupted. It seemed the least I could do.

Eric Bruhn
Ballet dancer

From the first moment I met Eric, I was mesmerized. I had seen him several times elegantly performing ballet classics, and he was equally riveting in person. Fueled by his warm conversation and beautiful presence, our initial meeting stretched out from cocktails at a party until many hours later walking home in the predawn light, brushing fingers and still talking. Other social encounters followed, though none matched the intensity of that first golden meeting. Eric always made me feel special.

17. Rita Hayworth, 1942

RITA HAYWORTH
Actress, dancer

I was dancing with Gilda. But it was an older, tired Gilda, Rita Hayworth a few years past her love goddess prime, and her distended belly pressed against my cummerbund as we shuffled around the floor.

"I knew one of your husbands," I said, trying to make conversation.

"Oh? Wish one?" she asked, her voice slurred.

"Ali Khan," I responded.

"Oh, him." She flapped her wrist in dismissal, but I felt her deep sadness.

The occasion was the wedding of Broadway producer Hal Prince to Judith Chaplin, daughter of Hollywood composer and musical director Saul Chaplin, in the fall of 1962, and many of the biggest names in show business were there. Rita and I decided we needed more room to show our stuff, and we purposely bumped other dancers off the floor and proceeded to execute a miserable attempt at an impromptu floor show. But sadly, we were not Mickey and Judy. We had no routine to offer. Gary Merrill finally got up and gently suggested to Rita that she rejoin him and Zero Mostel at their table. I was relieved and grateful for the termination of our ill-advised exhibition. To quote her famous song from *Gilda*, "Put the blame on Mame."

R. Eric Gustafson

18, Groucho Marx, 1947

GROUCHO MARX
Actor, comedian, game show host

In 1958, the summer before I went to Carnegie Tech (now Carnegie Mellon) to do graduate work in theater arts, I worked in summer stock at the Lakes Region Playhouse in Gilford, New Hampshire. Groucho Marx was appearing there in a play that season, and he invited some of us in the cast and crew to lunch at a nearby restaurant. A fan approached Groucho and extended his hand in greeting. Groucho covered his hand with a napkin and took the fan's in a shake. He proceeded to introduce his stage wife as his wife, despite the fact that his young, beautiful wife (the actress Eden Hartford) was sitting across the table. We were all amused. Wyatt Cooper was in that cast as well, and I had a warm relationship with him.

19. Veronica Lake, 1941

VERONICA LAKE
Actress

That same season, Veronica Lake appeared as Maggie in *Cat on a Hot Tin Roof* at the Lakes Region Playhouse. Although her husband had issued strict orders that "Ronnie" was not to have any alcohol, she surreptitiously arranged with me to sneak a beer backstage for her each evening. I liked her, but it was sad to see that so little of the luminous Veronica Lake I remembered, she of the famous peek-a-boo hairstyle, had survived the years since her heyday in Hollywood. She and her husband invited me to the house where they were staying one afternoon, which earned me some snide "starfucking" gibes from my jealous crew mates. I didn't care. I felt privileged to be accepted by this legendary film star.

20. Tallulah Bankhead as the Black Widow on Batman, 1967

Tallulah Bankhead
Actress

"Sonovabitch" was the nickname Tallulah Bankhead had for me at the playhouse that summer. Apparently I sounded a great deal like a New York friend of hers, and when she heard my voice backstage she thought it was him visiting. Alas, it was only me. "Sonovabitch!" she exclaimed. And so SOB it was. Tallulah was famous for taking off her clothes, and often her dressing room door was left open, to reveal her in all her wrinkled, sagging splendor. She kept her makeup on ice in an attempt to tighten her skin when applied, but the hot lights made short work of that effect. Tallulah's flamboyance, often fueled by bourbon, delighted me. The day before her opening in a play called *House on the Rocks* we waited at the playhouse for her to check the lighting (gels of bastard amber and lavender) and her props (boxes of English Craven "A" cigarettes, etc.). As befitted a star, she was hours late, but at last the doors burst open. In swept Tallulah, a mink coat draped over her shoulders despite the summer heat. She was accompanied by the town's police chief, who had provided her with a police escort after they met at a local bar where she'd stopped for a "pick-me-up." Tallulah tossed the fur over a seat and strode up onto the stage. It was a great entrance, and the beginning of two fabulous weeks together — *dah-lings!*

21. Jackie Kennedy, 1961

JACKIE KENNEDY
First Lady, editor

In the early Sixties I lived in the same 72nd Street building as the famous "Dr. Feelgood," Max Jacobs, purveyor of "miracle tissue regenerator" shots to the stars. His patient list was extensive and dazzling, but perhaps none was more famous that the President of the United States, John F. Kennedy. As I left my building one morning and started across the street I was startled to see Jacqueline Kennedy crossing toward me, flanked by two Secret Service agents. She fixed me with an intense gaze and a knowing smile. I was no stranger to being cruised, but this was unsettling, a blatant undressing with her eyes. Sadly, I was to discover that it wasn't only me — I later heard others had experienced this same look. In any case, I was not her destination. She was on her way that morning to the office of "Miracle Max," where her husband was getting shots to treat his severe chronic back pain.

I had received a splendid invitation to stay at a prominent Georgetown residence for Kennedy's inauguration, which promised to be a lively event with many glittering balls. Unfortunately, my finances would not permit the trip, and I missed out on a thrilling couple of days. However, I later did see the Kennedys in New York on several occasions.

22. Eric Gustafson with Bess and Harry S Truman, 1960 or 1961

Harry S Truman
President of the United States

During the brief Kennedy administration, the president and his wife took the upper three floors of the famed Carlyle Hotel on Madison Avenue (across from the Parke-Bernet Auction Galleries) for their New York presidential residence. The Kennedys had made it available to the Trumans while they were in the city visiting their daughter Margaret, who lived around the corner. It was there that I was invited by my partner David Wallace to meet former President Truman and his wife Bess (David was Bess Truman's nephew.) After some minutes of conversation Mrs. Truman offered us a glass of water. "A lot my girl knows," Truman laughed, taking me by the arm. "These boys don't want a drink of water!" He steered me into a small study which was complete with JFK's famous rocking chair, and a desk on which sat the hotline, the red phone that connected the President of the United States directly to the Kremlin and Premier Khrushchev. From behind a row of books Truman produced a square liquor bottle, and we proceeded to the kitchen for glasses. And thus began a warm relationship, and a new meaning for me to the tune, "I'm Just Wild About Harry."

Shortly after that, David and I visited Margaret Truman at the Park Avenue apartment she shared with her husband, the journalist Clifton Daniel, who was soon to become Managing Editor of the *New York Times*. I found him very sexy.

23. Lee Radziwill with Henry Kissinger
at the White House, 1974

Lee Radziwill
Princess, socialite

Jackie Kennedy's sister sat on my left at the elegant dinner party given in my honor by Lisa Taylor, Director of the Cooper-Hewitt Museum where I had just opened my exhibition of theater designs. Lee was a princess by way of her second marriage, to Prince Stanislaw Albrecht Radziwill, a Polish aristocrat. She was one of the most charming women I have ever met. She was stunning to look at, and enchanting to converse with. However, what I had read about Jackie pushing her out of Onassis's bed and taking her place popped into my mind during our lively conversation. She seemed so correct and proper. I realized that, as they say, a book's cover does not always reveal its contents, and a luminous exterior may disguise a very contrasting inner life.

24. Doris Duke, 1951

Doris Duke
Heiress, philanthropist, socialite

"May I join you?" Doris Duke, the tobacco heiress sometimes referred to as "the richest girl in the world," slid into the next chair at my table after dinner at the Bernardsville Mountain estate of fellow heiress and art collector Jane Engelhard. In contrast to the other ladies at the event, she wore a simple gown, with her hair pulled back in a ponytail. When I asked her to waltz, Doris accepted but warned me, "I might be rusty." She danced beautifully, and we turned up the next day under the byline of prominent New York Daily News society columnist Suzy Knickerbocker, who wrote "Eric Gustafson took the rust off Doris Duke, but left her her diamonds …" The diamonds in question were assembled into a spectacular necklace in a graduated series, with no attachments visible (similar in concept to a string of pearls) that cascaded into her ample cleavage. I was surprised at the areas her conversation covered, including a philanthropic concern for the poor in Newport, and an interest in Zen Buddhism. It seemed out of character for the woman who had famously crushed her lover to death with her car against the gates of her Newport mansion.

Grace Bumbry
Operatic soprano

"Let him in," came the voice from inside the locked door of the powder room. "Let him be the judge." It was my Colombian soul mate Ysabel Aya, who on the other side of the door was comparing breasts with the great African-American opera star Grace Bumbry. As distinguished opera personalities in formal attire mingled outside, I slipped into the inner sanctum and settled into my task of carefully surveying the bared breasts of the two formidable women. After an intense and difficult appraisal, I pronounced Grace the victor in the tit contest, gently placing a congratulatory kiss on the winning nipple.

This was the finale in a series of competitions between the diva and Ysabel, the woman who taught me to drink in the morning without guilt. It had begun weeks before, on the evening of the birthday party Ysabel threw for me at her floor-through Fifth Avenue apartment. When she arrived, I saw that Grace was wearing the multicolored sequined gown that she had worn at the farewell gala for the old Met on April 16th, 1966. I introduced her to Ysabel in the entrance hall. Ysabel mentioned that she had read in the *Times* that morning about the standing ovation Grace had received at the opera the night before. "Of course," she remarked, "I sing much better than you." I nearly fainted, but Grace surprised me by taking it in the playful spirit in which it was intended. Grace could be prickly, but she rose to this challenge, and it became the opening salvo in a friendly competition.

Navajo artist R. C. Gorman was at the party, and I introduced him to Grace. To my horror, he leaned forward and touched her bare shoulder. "Is this your real color?" he asked. I winced. Grace was extremely sensitive to racial slights. She glanced down at his finger, then looked him straight in the face. "Yes," she said. "Is that your real color?" *Touché!* The tone was set for a hilarious evening.

25. Grace Bumbry with Eric Gustafson

26. *Eric Gustafson (left) with Sir Harold Acton
in the formal palace gardens of La Pietra outside Florence*

Sir Harold Acton
Poet, author, historian, aesthete

At La Pietra, his estate just outside of Florence, Acton entertained on a lavish scale among his 18th century gardens and classical statuary. Sir Harold had been the prototype for Charles Ryder, the character portrayed by Jeremy Irons in the television miniseries based on Evelyn Waugh's novel *Brideshead Revisited*. I was fortunate to be included at luncheons there whenever I was in Florence.

27. Helen, Queen Mother of Romania, 1934

Queen Helen
Queen Mother of Romania

It was at one of Sir Harold's luncheon parties that I met Helen, the dowager queen of Romania during the reign of her son King Michael I. It was a gorgeous Tuscan afternoon, and after lunch the host invited his guests for a post-prandial stroll through his famous gardens. The aged queen begged off, preferring to sit in the enormous marbled hall rather than take the walking tour. I offered to keep her company. She remarked to me that from my gait and posture, she thought I must be in my twenties. Forgetting the cardinal rule about disagreeing with royalty, I told her I was in my forties. She was greatly distressed and began banging her cane on the marble floor, proclaiming loudly: "I am just a blind, silly old woman!" Sir Harold and some of his guests came rushing back to see what had happened. I was mortified.

28. Dame Joan Sutherland, photograph inscribed:
"For Eric — Best wishes, Joan Sutherland"

Dame Joan Sutherland
Operatic coloratura soprano

When David and I were living in Rome in 1962, we were fortunate to attend a recital by Joan Sutherland, the legendary Australian coloratura. It happened like this. The Richard Burton-Elizabeth Taylor epic *Cleopatra* was well into its chaotic production, and its leading actors were gifted with tickets to all the city's important cultural events. Burton's personal aide was an American friend of mine, and he passed on to me the tickets that the star wasn't using. How nice, I thought, after a hard day's shooting he prefers to return home to the Via Appia Antica for a quiet evening with his wife and children. I was wrong, as it turned out. A press telegram exposed the truth: "BURTON PLUCKING BRAINS OUT OF TAYLOR." In any case, David and I were the happy inheritors of the Burton tickets, and we were able to attend the first Joan Sutherland recital to be conducted by her husband, Richard Bonynge. Sutherland made a grand entrance in a green tulle gown that swept away every unguarded music stand in her path on her narrow approach to her downstage mark.

29. Beverly Sills, photograph inscribed: "To Eric — For his Hall of Fame — Love, Beverly Sills"

30. Joan Sutherland and Beverly Sills, in a rare appearance together, San Diego, 1980. Photograph inscribed to Eric Gustafson

BEVERLY SILLS
Operatic soprano

Sutherland appeared again to complicate my life nearly 20 years later, when the Australian diva shared the stage for the only time in their storied careers with American soprano Beverly Sills. The two were appearing in *Die Fledermaus* with the San Diego Opera in 1980. My exhibition of "Designs for a Prima Donna, Dame Joan Sutherland" was to open at Lincoln Center in October of that year. I had to go backstage to confer with Sutherland and Bonynge about various details pertaining to this enormous exhibition. I started worrying what to do if I were to meet both divas at the same time backstage. What was the protocol? Which of the illustrious stars should I greet first? Beverly by this time was a longtime friend, and had played hostess for me at one of my gallery galas. Joan was the subject of my impending exhibition. A blunder could be excruciating. I worked myself into a nervous knot.

Happily, the feared triangulation never took place. I met each soprano separately. Beverly would greet me with a hug and kiss. Joan would playfully deliver a butch punch to my shoulder.

Andy Warhol
Artist

I was seated in a helicopter squeezed between art collector Ethel Scull and Andy Warhol, flying over a stretch of Atlantic Ocean approaching Bridgehampton, Long Island. The mission was a publicity stunt for the opening of the Barge Disco there. We'd had a few drinks. And Andy was being a jerk.

"I have a good mind to push this pink-and-white asshole out over the ocean," I grumbled, reaching over Andy's crotch for the door handle.

Ethel put a restraining hand on my arm. "It's too good for him," she sniffed. "Every camera in the press below will capture his death for posterity." She patted my arm gently. "Too good for him," she said again.

Andy and I had had a peculiar relationship over the years. We'd known each other back when he was designing shoe promotions for a Fifth Avenue store. Our paths had intersected at various events in the city, usually art-related.

Before he moved to the Union Square "factory," I visited his Upper East Side apartment. His plump Polish mother, clad in a housecoat, was standing at the kitchen sink signing his name to the back of one of his paintings. "Her handwriting is better than mine," Warhol commented. He led me into the bedroom to show me something. I was fascinated by a set of wig stands on top of one of his bedroom armoires. All the wigs were in various states of disarray.

His later disruptive behavior alienated me. Which brings us back to the helicopter bound for Bridgehampton, when I had the notion to push him out. But gratefully, Ethel's calming presence intervened, and we landed and disembarked to exploding flash bulbs. I never saw Andy again.

31. Andy Warhol, 1973

32. Alvin Ailey, 1975. Photograph inscribed: "For Eric — Because he is who he is — and quite quite divinely crazy!"

ALVIN AILEY
Dancer, choreographer, dance company founder

The Waltz Series is the most elite dance group in New York, a formal and elegant celebration of the spirit of late 19th century Vienna. I was preparing to attend, and Alvin was helping me get into my white tie and tails, when another thought crossed my mind. "What if we reversed this dressing process, and headed instead for the sheeted fields?" I suggested suggestively. Alvin laughed. "Whatever would we do there?" he countered. It was a witty evasion of my proposal, and we amicably completed the finishing touches on my attire as we discussed details of a costume exhibit I was preparing for him. I admired Alvin greatly, and he was fond of me too, but his sexual preference was for young ruffians.

33. Greta Garbo, 1930

Greta Garbo
Actress

"You could be my nephew!" Garbo exclaimed when I told her my name. "Gustafsson was my name before I changed it." We were in the Parke-Bernet Auction Galleries, across from the Carlyle Hotel. I was employed there during much of the 1960s. Parke-Bernet had a rarified atmosphere, frequented by elegant ladies sporting their finest. In sharp contrast, Garbo would appear there in a shapeless old raincoat and rainhat, wearing sneakers and white socks. She adored looking at lovely things, but dressed to her own drummer. On this occasion she had spotted me from across the room. "Who is that beautiful young man?" she demanded of the manager, who was always at her elbow. He called me over, we were introduced, and the congruence of our surnames cemented a friendship.

Anthony Perkins
Actor

I arrived in Rome during my first foray into Europe at the tail end of a shoestring budget. It was the late Fifties, I had just graduated from Queens college, and I was soaking in old-world culture. Unfortunately I was almost broke, and it occurred to me that I might improve my finances by heading out to Cinecittá and finding work as an extra. I had read in the *Rome Daily American* that Anthony Perkins was shooting a film. So I made my way there and managed to sneak in. Wandering the hallways, I opened a door and came face to face with Sir Michael Redgrave. He was in full costume and makeup, ready to head out to the set. He suggested I wait there for his return. Sensing his intentions, I felt very uneasy, and when I was discovered by a security guard I was happy to leave.

Shortly thereafter I came upon Tony Perkins, who was taking a break with a few other actors. I introduced myself and told him why I was there.

"Take off those dark glasses," he suggested. I did. "That's better. They want to be able to see your eyes." He called over someone who could arrange my employment as an extra, starting the next day.

We lived in the same neighborhood near the Spanish Steps, but somehow we made each other nervous. When I spotted him on the Via Condotti I would cross the street to avoid an awkward encounter.

Twenty years later, at Mia Farrow's Valentine dinner dance, I would get to thank him for helping me to survive my first Roman holiday. I ran into Berry Berenson, Tony's wife, who told me he was there. I asked her to see if he'd stop by my table when he had a chance. He did. Whatever awkwardness we'd felt before had disappeared, and I expressed my gratitude for his long-ago help. Tony died of AIDS in 1992. A decade later, Berry perished in one of the planes that crashed into the World Trade Center on 9/11.

34. *Anthony Perkins with Mia Farrow*

R. Eric Gustafson

35. Edward Mulhare, circa 1968,
in a publicity photograph for The Ghost and Mrs. Muir

36. Jennie Tourel, circa 1943

Edward Mulhare
Actor

Jennie Tourel
Operatic mezzo-soprano

O ver Christmas break from Carnegie Tech in 1958, I was invited by my friend Noel Davis to stay at the New York apartment he was sharing with Edward Mulhare, who had taken over from Rex Harrison as Professor Higgins in *My Fair Lady.* Noel was Mulhare's aide-de-camp. Rounding out the apartment's residents was Jean Susskind, wife of the conductor Walter Susskind and Mulhare's current fling.

My wife of less than a year was unable to get work leave, so I kissed her goodbye and merrily set off for the Big Apple. Shortly after I arrived, Noel included me in an invitation to tea with Jennie Tourel, the noted mezzo-soprano, at her apartment. It was a delightful afternoon filled with stories from her illustrious career, and it culminated with an invitation to a supper party she was hosting for her dear friend, the fast-rising superstar of American music, Leonard Bernstein.

LEONARD BERNSTEIN
Musician, composer, conductor

Bernstein had just returned from a hugely successful Russian tour, and New York had fêted him with a ticker tape parade on Fifth Avenue. Lennie was the talk of the town and I was tingling with anticipation. En route to the event, Noel, Jean, and I discussed how delightful it would be if we could engage Lennie in a foursome. Mulhare was unable to attend, but sent with Noel a copy of the *Times of London* which had a review of *West Side Story* that Bernstein was eager to read.

I knew that the guest of honor would be deluged by well-wishers, so I decided that if I was to get his attention I would have to play it very cool. When we arrived, Lennie saw us and strolled over. As Noel greeted him and gave him the newspaper, I purposely turned my back on him.

"Who's the guy?" Bernstein asked, and I knew I had hit my mark.

As the evening was drawing to a close, Noel, Jean, and I discussed possible outcomes. Noel thought Lennie wanted a foursome. Jean thought he wanted a threesome. But under the tablecloth, Lennie's fingers probing my upper thigh told me that he did not want a foursome nor a threesome, but a twosome!

Lennie took Jean, Noel, me, and a few determined Russian partiers to his studio for a pre-dawn night cap. As Lennie had a matinee concert at Carnegie Hall later that day, he finally managed to free himself for some much-needed shut-eye. Noel and I were invited to sit in his box for the concert. In the Green Room after-

A Path Lit by Stars

ward, the maestro asked where he could reach me later to arrange some time alone. I had had to relocate from the Mulhare apartment, as Noel's nose was out of joint over Bernstein's attentions to me. Lennie memorized my new contact number and called me later that afternoon.

37. Leonard Bernstein

38. *Virgil Thomson reviewing a score with Gertrude Stein, circa 1929*

Virgil Thompson
Composer, critic

"You can't fool me," said a bemused Virgil Thompson, fingering the elaborate arrangement of silver flatware with which I had dressed the table. Honored that this world-famous composer had accepted my luncheon invitation, and knowing his love of excellent wines, I had made that the focus of the meal. I was serving only a Colombian stew and dessert to compliment the wine selections. The table would have looked dismally bare if I'd only laid down a soup spoon and a dessert spoon, which was all the meal called for. So I put on a show, with an army of flatware dazzling amidst fine crystal, and all set off with flowers. The dapper Thompson, who was accustomed to far more elevated circumstances than my modest New York apartment, looked it all over. And he did seem perplexed, and yes, fooled, by my eccentric hosting.

39. Zsa Zsa Gabor, 1959

Zsa Zsa Gabor
Actress, socialite

My two encounters with the Hungarian beauty (famous chiefly for being famous) were glancing and widely spaced in time and place. The first was West Coastal. I was ringing the bell on the garden gate of a friend in Chautauqua Canyon when a blue Cadillac convertible pulled up behind me. "Eez he home?" inquired a voice. I turned to see a butch woman at the wheel and the unmistakable, glamorous Zsa Zsa in the passenger seat. I shrugged. "Tell heem I vas here," she said, raising her dark glasses to gaze at me with her big blue eyes. I suppressed the naughty impulse to ask who she was.

"I certainly will," I said.

Some years later, I was enjoying a post-performance nightcap after the Metropolitan Opera at the elegant Peacock Alley in the Waldorf Astoria with several bejeweled and distinguished ladies. Zsa Zsa walked by, on the arm of Huntington Hartford. I knew Hunt from the New York eligible bachelor party circuit we both frequented. As he stopped to greet me, Zsa Zsa's eyes appraised the jewels of my companions. She then turned her knowing glance on me, and smiled with approval.

40. Robert Indiana, 2013

Robert Indiana
Artist

At a gala opening at the Guggenheim Museum I came face to face with Robert Indiana, he of the iconic LOVE imagery. "I've been meaning to be in touch with you," he said, seeming a trifle flustered. I assured him not to worry, we'd catch up soon, and we went our separate mingling ways. It was not till some time later, on an evening when I was visiting Robert Lynn Batts Tobin at his Park Avenue townhouse, that it dawned on me why Indiana had seemed so awkward that day. Tobin showed me a handsome catalogue of his acquisition of Indiana's complete drawings for *Mother of Us All*, that had been produced at the Santa Fe Opera. At the time, Indiana had discussed with me his interest in selling the collection. I thought of Tobin, whom I had been advising over the years on his art collection, and brought the drawings to his attention. Nothing more was said about it. But when I realized that Indiana had made the sale to Tobin for $490,000, I calculated that my commission should be in the neighborhood of $49,000. No wonder he had been embarrassed to see me at the Guggenheim! Time had passed, and Indiana was not responding to my letters to his Maine island retreat. I knew it was useless to pursue it further. His last years were spent as a reclusive millionaire. LOVE indeed.

41. Dennis Hopper, 1973

DENNIS HOPPER
Actor

When Dennis Hopper bought the fabled Mabel Dodge Lujan property in Taos in the early Seventies, it became a lively place for revelers to enjoy abandoned pleasures of sex, drugs. and alcohol. On occasion, I had accepted invitations to these saturnalias. When the Santa Fe gossip columnist Calla Hay wrote in the *New Mexican* that I would be flying in on a private plane from Los Angeles to introduce my beautiful English friend Allegra Kent Taylor and her newly minted husband Douglas Campbell to the charms of Taos, Hopper invited us to a private viewing of *Easy Rider*. He owned the now dark movie house in Rancho de Taos, but he had it opened for our private viewing, and he even gave us a fine lunch before the screening. How remarkable is that?

March 27, 1995

Dear Eric,

    Thank you for your long lost letter which I finally recieved and for the wonderful article that you wrote. You have been so kindly attentive over the years and I appreciate it very much.

    It's always wonderful to see all the terrific things that you are doing and with such gusto as well.

    Thanks for many kindesses to me.

    Lots of love,

42. *Frederica von Stade, along with a letter to Eric Gustafson dated March 27, 1995*

Frederica von Stade
Operatic mezzo-soprano

This lovely lady entered my life on the back of one of Winnebelle Beasley's horses as we rode in Tesuque, outside of Santa Fe. On Sundays, when the Santa Fe Opera was dark, Winnie led trail rides up and around the arroyos and foothills. "Flicka" and I often brought up the rear, perhaps because we were experienced riders who did not need instruction. This gentle young woman was to become a major international star, but she never lost her modestly and warm charm. I have been a huge fan for years, and I treasure a note she sent me in 1995: "You have been so kindly attentive over the years and I appreciate it very much. It is always wonderful to see all the terrific things you are doing and with such gusto as well. Thanks for many kindnesses to me. Lots of love, Flicka."

43. Wyatt Cooper and Gloria Vanderbilt, 1964

WYATT COOPER
Author, screenwriter, actor

Good-hearted, handsome, and with an easy southern charm, Wyatt Cooper entranced me that summer of 1958 that I spent at the Lakes Region Playhouse in New Hampshire. He was in the cast of *Time for Elizabeth,* the play that starred Groucho Marx, and it was a thrilling time for me. After the season, I left for a European trip. On my return, I had a big surprise. The front page of the *New York Daily News* was splashed with a large picture of my Georgia peach. He had married Gloria Vanderbilt, the "poor little rich girl."

GLORIA VANDERBILT
Heiress, socialite, author, artist

She always wore white make-up and never seemed to be having much fun. She was stand-offish and imperious. Her studio was in the building next to my apartment on 72nd Street near Fifth Avenue, so I would often bump into Wyatt and Gloria when he came to pick her up. Later, after they had two boys, I sometimes encountered him walking with them around their home near UN Plaza. Wyatt was invariably agreeable, polite, and most attractive. I have always enjoyed my memories of our time together during that distant summer of stock theater. Someday, I would like to share this with Anderson, his famous newscaster son.

44. Samuel Barber, 1944

SAMUEL BARBER
Composer, pianist

"I wouldn't mind taking up residence here," the elegant, pleasant-mannered gentleman at my side remarked. We were standing on the terrace of a grand ancient palace overlooking the town of Spoleto, with its beautiful piazza and venerable cathedral. The gentleman was the great composer Samuel Barber, and the fantasy of having this wonderful man as my neighbor appealed to me, even though it was said strictly in jest.

"Nor would I," I agreed.

Barber had a male companion at his side, and I was there with two English colleagues who were to assist me in running a theater design gallery in conjunction with the Festival of Two Worlds, the brainchild of Gian Carlo Menotti, Barber's former lover, and still a close friend.

Gian Carlo Menotti
Composer, librettist, director, festival founder

Menotti wanted me to mount a theater design exhibition at his Festival of Two Worlds in Spoleto. The quality of the exhibits had slipped over the seasons. He had been impressed by the tribute that I had created in New York honoring the old Metropolitan Opera, and saluting the newly constructed Met at Lincoln Center. He wooed me with many attractive promises to help me make this venture viable.

A delightful gallery space was provided for me to exhibit original costume and scenic designs for opera, ballet, and theater. Glittering personages from the performing arts and international society would mingle, stars like Ingrid Bergman and Anna Magnani, amicably conversing with champagne glasses in hand while viewing the theater art displayed on the gallery walls. After hours, I enjoyed the attentions of beguiling Italians, and on occasion, I indulged in late-night escapades with a dashing nobleman in a speeding sports car.

This enterprise was not to have a happy ending. I had been advised by my partners that to avoid taxes and complications, all monies were to be banked in England. At the end of the festival, I would meet them in London and we would divide up the considerable profits. When I arrived both partners met me at the airport and took me to an inexpensive restaurant for lunch. I began to suspect that something was amiss. They explained to me that the costs of the Spoleto venture had canceled out any profit. There was nothing left over for me. I could have put up a stink, but I could see it was no use.

I returned to Taormina, where I had just spent some blissful vacation days with my wonderful new David, David II. I had left Sicily a prince, and returned a pauper.

After some months of recuperation, I flew back to New York, where I ran into some people who had lost their gallery director and wanted me to take over their operation. When I looked at the space and realized that I could use the room at the back for exhibits of original costume and scenic designs, I accepted with that provision. I opened my gallery of designs just weeks before my English ex-partners opened theirs in New York.

Some time later I returned to Spoleto with my dear friend Ysabel Aya to show her the festival. I introduced Ysabel to Menotti at an opera after-party at the Renaissance palazzo he occupied overlooking Spoleto. Eager to charm a potential supporter of the festival, and hearing that Ysabel was born in Colombia, he told her that his mother was Colombian, too. "Yes, I know," she replied, "she was our cook."

45. *Gian Carlo Menotti (right) with Willem de Kooning, along with an accompanying note to Ysabel*

46. Gustav III, 1777

47. Queen Sylvia, 2023

King Gustav III
King of Sweden

Queen Sylvia
Queen of Sweden

A most prestigious and fabulous summer was that of 1969. I departed New York for Sweden where the Queen had granted me some days in residence at Gripsholm Castle to do research on King Gustav III, an 18th century Swedish ruler. He was featured in a book I was writing on the Court Theaters of Europe. I knew two of the curators, who provided me a delightful time there. A very gay dinner was given in my honor to which outstanding scholars from various Swedish institutions were in attendance. I gave a most impish after-dinner speech that ruffled the more conservative guests.

Ysabel was waiting for me in Rome, where we were fêted by some local nobility before moving onto Spoleto. We rented a charming small house surrounded by fields of poppies on the outskirts of this delightful town. I wanted Ysabel to enjoy the diverse cultural activities presented by Maestro Gian Carlo Menotti. A few years earlier, I had produced a theater design exhibition there, and I wanted to indulge again in that lively atmosphere.

48. Willem de Kooning in his studio, 1961

Willem de Kooning
Artist

Early one morning on that return visit with Ysabel to Spoleto, I found myself wandering the empty piazza in front of the Duomo. It was a sunny, lovely morning, and I sat down near the steps in front of the church soaking in the sun, Renaissance history, and Italian beauty of this gorgeous Umbrian town. After a few moments, another straggler appeared. To my surprise and delight, I recognized the artist Willem de Kooning. An exhibition of his work was on view in Spoleto. I felt honored and thrilled to be in his presence. However, I did not mention anything about his work or the exhibition. We sat there, quietly absorbing the atmosphere.

After a while, I mentioned that my friend and I were giving an afternoon gathering that day at our modest country retreat, and would be pleased if he would join us. De Kooning reminded me of a shy rabbit, somewhat uneasy with the world around him. However, he seemed pleased by my invitation and said he would be glad to attend. Just then, a couple of people appeared. They seemed to be keeping an eye on him, but he had momentarily eluded them. He bid me a sad farewell as he was led away.

49. *Gayelord Hauser, 1961*

GAYELORD HAUSER
Nutrition writer

D avid and I were standing on Taormina's Lettoyani beach when we noticed a small motorboat approaching. In it were a few young men I knew from the Spoleto Festival, the actor John Philip Law among them. We waved.

"It seems you know my guests," said the owner of the nearby villa. It was Gayelord Hauser, the nutritionist and health writer. "Please join us for lunch."

David and I introduced ourselves to this famous consultant to the stars, and gladly accepted the invitation. We ditched our paper bag lunch and prepared to dine well and healthily. Hauser was well-known for his mingling with movie royalty and advising them on health and diet. And now it was our turn to sample his hospitality. Sadly, I was to abuse it. This was in my heavy drinking days, and my alcohol consumption turned me arrogant and rude at lunch. What could have been a very agreeable relationship was soured beyond repair.

50. Elizabeth Taylor, in her dressing room with Eric Gustafson

Elizabeth Taylor
Actress

"Get your ass over to Betty Ford's!" Elizabeth Taylor was lecturing artist R. C. Gorman at his house in Taos, but I took the command to heart. Recognizing that what she said applied equally to me, I not only heard this advice, I immediately followed it. She was not the first to impress upon me how much I needed help with my out-of-control drinking. I spilled more than most people drank. But what did those do-gooders know? However, when the Empress of the Cinema speaks, I pay attention. This was an instance when my absorption with celebrity paid dividends in my favor. I called the Betty Ford Center to arrange my admittance. And it changed my life.

Years later, Elizabeth invited R. C. and me to attend her performance in *The Little Foxes* on Broadway. In her dressing room afterwards, I was tempted to mention something about my being in Rome for her torrid affair with Burton during the filming of *Cleopatra*, but she quickly shut down that topic. It reminded me of Sutherland smoothly ignoring any reference to her pulling down the music stands at her Rome recital. Both women reflected a steely, disciplined professionalism in maintaining their image.

R. C. GORMAN
Artist

"You should see the autograph I gave Eric on his bottom," the jovial and very drunk R. C. crowed to the blue-haired matron who had approached our table to get his signature on his exhibition brochure. We were dining in Santa Fe's elegant Palace restaurant.

"Can I see it?" she asked.

"For two dollars," I impishly replied.

She promptly opened her purse and laid two crisp bills on the table.

I rose, and slipped my custom-made blue chiffon Stavropoulos trousers down just enough to reveal my inscribed left cheek.

Shortly thereafter, another fine lady approached and put a couple of dollars on the table. And then another. I was delighted with my sudden windfall, and foresaw an easy road to riches. Unfortunately, a little later after a steamy interlude, I took a shower, and carelessly washed away my meal ticket. I should have sat on a Xerox machine!

R. C. once engaged me to take him and his nephew, who had never been off the reservation, on a tour of Rome, Florence, and Venice. The proviso was threefold: he wanted to meet a nobleman, he wanted to meet a famous actress, and he wanted an audience with the Pope. In addition, I was to educate his nephew about the Italian Renaissance. I was currently involved with a young duke who lent us his car while we were in Rome, and we dined with a count and countess. One down. We got lost driving around Sophia Loren's residence, which we agreed counted. Two. And we were able to join a group assembled for a Papal audience. Mission accomplished! And I conscientiously filled the eager nephew's head with the history and culture of the Renaissance, and quizzed him from time to time. He was an apt student.

51. Elizabeth Taylor with R. C. Gorman

52. Betty Ford, 1990

Betty Ford
First Lady, founder of the Betty Ford Clinic

After leaving the White House, the former First Lady had publicly disclosed her struggles with alcohol and substance abuse, and sought help. When she recovered, she established a center to help others with similar problems. Elizabeth Taylor had been one of her first patients. I subscribed wholeheartedly to the program while in residence, and had the privilege of enjoying a warm relationship with this endearing, wholesome mentor.

I marveled at her persistent leadership, wondering how this fragile woman could maintain her vigor. When I hugged her, I could feel every rib in her slim body. She thanked me for creating the *All New Nativity Play* at the Christmas celebration, and said it was the happiest Christmas in the center's history. She invited me to come back anytime.

53. Catherine Deneuve, at the Sherry-Netherland dinner-dance with Eric Gustafson

CATHERINE DENEUVE
Actress

"What was she like?" my friend asked me.
"The lights were on," I replied, "but no one was home."

The lady in question was the fabled French superstar Catherine Deneuve, who had skyrocketed to fame in *Umbrellas of Cherbourg* in 1964, and gone on to be acclaimed over a long career as one of the leading ladies of film. The occasion was an Anglo-French dinner-dance at New York's Sherry-Netherland hotel. Mlle. Deneuve was there to represent France. I was the escort for Dorothy Dillon Eweson, whose brother Douglas had served as America's ambassador to France. The Dillons, who were there on behalf of the United States, owned Château Haut-Brion, producers of the finest Bordeaux wine. It was a brilliant social event, highlighted by the appearance of the great Deneuve, who chain-smoked thin cigarettes and had little to say. I suppose it was her duty to represent her country, but she wasn't able to muster much enthusiasm for this assignment.

54. Holly Woodlawn, with note to Eric Gustafson:
"Eric, Thank you for that fabulous photo, Love Holly"

Holly Woodlawn
Warhol superstar

"You are no gentleman!" she exclaimed, slapping my face as I stood naked in the doorway of my walk-up apartment.

"And you are no lady!" I countered, and slammed the door on the Warhol drag queen.

Holly and I had explored alcohol-fueled interludes a couple of times, but despite our best efforts we couldn't make a go of it. Watching her give Joe Dallesandro a blow job in the opening scene of Warhol's *Trash* was far more satisfying than anything we engaged in.

55. Andrew Robert the 11th Duke of Devonshire

THE DUKE OF DEVONSHIRE
British peer

The Cavendish family is one of the most prominent names in the British peerage, and has held the title of Duke of Devonshire since the 16th century. So when I introduced my boyfriend Rupert Cavendish and his socially ambitious mother Hazel, the Duke was understandably befuddled.

"You must be one of the American Cavendishes," he said, extending an aristocratic hand.

It was the opening day at the Royal Academy of an exhibition of theater designs created centuries earlier by Inigo Jones for the Stuarts' masques. I held the invitation from the Duke, written on his crested paper that he recognized as I approached him. When he saw the letter in my hand the Duke greeted us cordially. However, his suggestion that she must be of an American branch of Cavendishes crushed Hazel to the core. We who knew her were vastly amused.

56. *John XXIII, in an undated photograph released by the Vatican in 2010*

John XXIII
Pope

"Who would like to speak in French?" the pope asked as we stood piously around him. He had looked pale and serious when he entered this Vatican reception room, but as he warmed up the color came into his cheeks, and I began to suspect he forgot about being Pope. His good humor had earned him the nickname of "Jolly John," and once, when asked by a reporter how many people worked at the Vatican, he quipped, "Oh, about half of them." This great man who hosted a long overdue Ecumenical Council was a powerful example of exerting change through humility.

57. *Lillian Gish, in* Way Down East *(1920)*

Lillian Gish
Actress

The note read "Congratulations on your deserved success. Ever fondly, Lillian Gish." This was in response to my sending her a program for an upcoming event at my Apollo Muses Center for the Arts. We had discussed it several days earlier when we had met at the Fifth Avenue apartment of a bishop of the Episcopalian church. As I entered, I saw that the famous eyes of Lillian Gish were fixed upon me. She gestured for me to sit next to her. We had never met, but we had friends in common. I spent the cocktail hour conversing with this living legend. She seemed interested in my Apollo Muses cultural series. Some correspondence resulted which is now in my archive at the Bienecke Library at Yale University.

58. Greer Garson, 1940s

GREER GARSON
Actress

"Hello, I'm Greer Garson," the famed film star said, taking my hand.

Of course, you are, I thought.

I introduced myself, and we chatted about Santa Fe and the Southwest and art. We were guests at a private party in La Fonda Hotel, across the street from the prestigious Jamison Galleries where I was the director. Greer was married to Buddy Fogelson, owner of Forked Lightning Ranch in the Pecos. She was beautiful and charming, but she had a reputation for expecting a cut rate for anything she purchased. When she indicated her interest in a large Wilson Hurley painting that was displayed in our gallery window, my heart sank. The picture was of a cottonwood tree along the Rio Grande River. Miss Garson wondered if the artist would paint a figure under the tree, as she felt it was lacking in human interest. With all the tact I could muster, I explained this was something that the artist would not be willing to do. I was relieved when the matter was dropped.

59. James Baldwin, 1969

James Baldwin
Writer

It was the summer of 1963, and I had taken a break from my duties at Parke-Bernet to visit a friend at The Pines on Fire Island, which was a beacon for people in the arts, and particularly gays. When I dropped in after lunch that day I was blown away to discover that his luncheon guest was James Baldwin.

Baldwin had achieved enormous fame both as an author and for his civil rights activism. I was embarrassed that of all his works I had read only *Giovanni's Room,* so I steered the conversation to other subjects. He had a ferry to catch in a couple of hours, but we had plenty of time for conversation as we walked around the wooden raised paths in the Pines. He talked about the problems he was having as a Black man finding suitable housing in New York City. After some thought, I suggested looking into an apartment house on upper Central Park West that seemed to accommodate a mixture of races. James Baldwin displayed a warm friendliness that contrasted with the angry, confrontational image with which he is often identified. I remember with fondness our quiet afternoon together at the Pines that summer.

60. Leslie Caron, 1953

LESLIE CARON
Actress, dancer

Several decades after she won my heart as the adorable gamine in *An American in Paris* and *Gigi,* I met Leslie Caron in a conference room at the American Church in Paris. She was chairing a meeting at which I was the guest speaker. Her gentle modesty and warm responsiveness to my talk endeared her to me all over again. I was impressed with her very French attention to detail in presentation: make-up, hair, demure but smart outfit complete with alligator shoes. Our conversation after the meeting led me to think she was willing to continue our talk, but I wanted to avoid any possible complications that might result, and so I bid her a very fond farewell. I admire her tremendously.

61. Jean-Louis Barrault in Les Enfants du Paradis (1945)

JEAN-LOUIS BARRAULT
Actor, director, mime

The great Jean-Louis Barrault came to New York City in the Seventies to direct *Carmen* at the Met. I remembered him as Bip in Marcel Carné's classic film *Les Enfants du Paradis*. Later, he and his wife, Madeleine Renaud, created a theater in what had been the Gare d'Orsay (now the Musée d'Orsay). It was an unwieldy space. I saw Renaud perform there in a French translation of *Tea and Sympathy*. Barrault was planning to attend a small gathering at my friend Yvette's Park Avenue penthouse. He had expressed an interest in trying marijuana, so Yvette promised to invite a few people over to smoke pot.

I was the only person in this young collection of "beautiful people" who knew anything about this great French actor. He was grateful to have someone to converse with. Standing by his side as the small library filled with pot smoke, I began to feel as though a huge sunflower was growing out of my head. It got so heavy that I lay down on the floor to let it grow along the rug. Looking up, I noted with great joy that Barrault was performing a marvelous mime that only I was aware of. It was a great gift to me, I thought.

62. Jane Goodall, 2019

Jane Goodall
Primatologist, ethnologist, anthropologist

In my copy of her book *Reason for Hope*, the legendary primatologist wrote "Thank you for your help, Jane Goodall." We were both appearing at the Chautauqua Institution in upstate New York, to promote our newly published books. She had an attractive young assistant with her. I joined their efforts to prepare for the enormous turnout that would attend her talk and book signing, and she appreciated my assistance. I was thrilled to meet and spend time with this modest living legend. She will be sorely missed.

63. Alexandra "Choura" Danilova with Eric Gustafson

ALEXANDRA DANILOVA
Ballerina assoluta, *choreographer*

"I was, how you say ... his common wife," the *ballerina assoluta* explained in her Russian accent. She had had a long and intimate relationship with choreographer George Balanchine. They left Russia together in 1924, and both soon joined Sergei Diaghilev's *Ballets Russes*. After Diaghilev's death in '29, Danilova joined the *Ballet Russe de Monte Carlo*. Most ballerinas do not make good social dancers. "Choura" was the exception. I enjoyed waltzing with her more than anyone else. Her graceful ease and elegance, combined with lively conversation and fascinating reminiscences made escorting her a pleasure. At a formal dinner party this lovely dancer astonished the guests by kneeling and kissing the hand of Tennessee Williams, to whom she had just been introduced. It was her very Russian way of paying respect to the great playwright.

64. Tennessee Williams

TENNESSEE WILLIAMS
Playwright

Tennessee was often in attendance at the social events I went to. Movie premieres, discos, and gay-oriented gatherings were magnets for him. I would always see him alone, sedately dressed, quietly observing with a gentle smile. It was remarkable that this slightly pudgy middle-aged man was the mind behind plays like *Cat on a Hot Tin Roof* and *The Glass Menagerie*, searing dramas that shook the American theater. He kept a suite at the Hotel Elysée on East 54th Street when he was in New York. It was there that he signed his autobiographical work *Memoirs* for me. And it was there that he was found dead some years later, in 1983.

R. Eric Gustafson

Mae West
Actress

In the 1933 film *She Done Him Wrong*, Mae West purrs seductively to Cary Grant "Why dontcha come up and see me sometime?" That famous line inspired the mural of life-sized nude men climbing the staircase leading to the bedrooms in her Santa Monica beach home. Their muscled, flesh-toned bodies sported large, gilded erections. This scene, running the length of the staircase, greeted visitors as they entered the front door. The unabashed provocation was typical for Mae.

She used the beach house as a getaway from Ravenswood, her primary residence in the Hollywood hills. Now it was for sale, and Mae usually came to visit on Thursdays. The realtor was a friend of mine who invited me to come down and have a look. Everything in the house had once been white. Time had turned it all beige, yellowish or gray. The only bright spot was an obviously new white shawl, artfully draped on a chaise lounge in her bedroom. Looking around, there was nothing that a souvenir seeker would want. The cheap cross and bobby pin with plastic butterfly attached lying in a *cache pot* on her dressing table seemed hardly worth the effort to collect. Only the small framed pencil sketch of a naked woman lying spreadeagled on a boulder, hanging on the wall at the bottom of the stairway, was tempting. It was inscribed "Mae West 1935."

As I was starting to leave I got a thrilling surprise. Mae was there! She had been occupied on the ground floor while I was inspecting the bedrooms. Her black Cadillac was waiting outside the front door. As she headed towards it, Mae turned and saw me. I felt like Cary Grant as she appraised me in her inimitable fashion. Her driver opened the rear door for her. As she climbed in, the long dress she was wearing shifted up to expose painted toenails peeking from an elevated golden sandal. As she settled, the gown slid higher to reveal another foot on another platformed sandal. Mae West had lost some height with her advancing years. Wearing short stilts gave her the appearance of being taller. Her hair was pulled up on top of her head to add a few more inches. What a show woman!

65. *Mae West. Photo inscribed:*
"To Eric Sin-cerely"

WILLIAM HURT
Actor

As the AA meeting I was attending one evening in Paris broke up, the young man with a cap pulled down over his eyes approached me. "Don't tell the family I'm here," he said. It was Bill Hurt, by now a famous movie star. I assured him I would respect his privacy.

Hurt, the step-grandson of my dear friend Lila Tyng, was an on-and-off visitor to Lu Shan, her gorgeous estate in New Jersey. It had been built by her first husband, Henry Luce, publisher of *Time* magazine, for Lila and their two young sons.

Luce never spent a night there. Clare Boothe beckoned, and he followed. Henry, the son of Presbyterian missionaries, was strongly identified with the church, which frowned on divorce, and his split with his wife created a scandal. It was (to that point) the American Divorce of the Century.

When Lila and Henry's eldest, Henry III, married Claire Isabel Hurt, he adopted her sons William and James. William grew up adoring Lila, and visited whenever possible. His acting success grew, taking him from the New York stage to international acclaim in Hollywood.

Bill always enjoyed his Lu Shan visits and expressed pleasure in knowing that I was there for Lila. On a few occasions, he invited Lila and me to attend a performance of his on Broadway, followed by a dinner full of warm conversation. As his movie career took off, there was little time for New Jersey visits, but he kept in close touch with Lila. I telephoned him expressing joy when he won the Oscar for his role in *Kiss of the Spider Woman* in 1985.

Bill was a quiet, damaged soul who found escape through acting. He was comfortable around Lila, and admired her. His relationship with his stepfather, and Henry's wives after his mother died, was disagreeable and hostile. I was glad for his kindnesses to me. Bill's death in 2022 surprised everyone, but I believe he has now found a long sought-for peace.

66. William Hurt

R. Eric Gustafson

Martha Mitchell
Wife of Nixon's Attorney General

Truman Capote
Writer

"Please, do not take my picture!" the lady I was dancing with called out to the photographers gathered at the edge of the floor. This amused me as I don't think any of the paparazzi had recognized the wife of Nixon's powerful Attorney General John Mitchell until she drew attention to herself. Martha was an attractive woman, and a compulsive gabber. She was rattling on to me about Camp David, where she had been bored to death, but still absorbed much of what was going on.

Shortly after this MOMA fundraiser, in May of 1976 news broke of Martha's death. The official cause was multiple myeloma, but the rumor around town was that she had been given a lethal transfusion for her ailing back. Martha had been spilling information about Watergate and the shady doings of the president and his aides. She had shown Woodward and Bernstein some of her husband's papers, saying "Please nail him. I hope you get the bastard."

The songbird had been silenced.

Truman Capote had been living in Oliver Smith's basement apartment, but then moved to United Nations Plaza. I had the off-putting experience of meeting him there late one evening. I had escorted Alice Fordyce home. She lived on a floor beneath this famous writer. I said goodnight and rang for the elevator. When the door opened, a very inebriated Capote was slouched within. He eyed me, and gestured that I should get in. Using crude and vulgar expressions, he indicated that he wanted me to ascend with him to his apartment above. With utter disgust, I ignored him and let the elevator door close. As a beautiful youth, Capote captured the world's attention with his *Other Voices, Other Rooms* and subsequent books like *Breakfast at Tiffany's* and *In Cold Blood.* Later in life, he was ostracized by society for his revelations of intimate information confided to him by his "swans," the women who had been his friends in New York's high society. He died a broken man.

67. *Truman Capote and Martha Mitchell, 1975*

68. *Edward Albee, 1975*

Edward Albee
Playwright

For a couple of years in the Sixties, David the First and I rented a small house on the middle dune on the east end of the Pines. Edward Albee was often on the same ferry to Fire Island. He would continue trudging along the beach eastward to an isolated area, long since abandoned. We knew each other from his art interests. For a brief period I had worked at Brentano's, and Albee came to investigate School of Paris works that the Galerie Moderne was showing there. It was a large red conté drawing attributed to Renoir of a nude youth that drew his return visits. Albee arranged a ticket for me to *A Delicate Balance,* his current play on Broadway, where I was delighted to be seated next to the music critic from the *New York Times,* a friend of mine from East Hampton. Albee later shifted his beach getaway from the Pines to the tip of Long Island, just past Amagansett. We had a friend in common there and would cross paths occasionally with minimal conversation. Albee was notoriously solitary.

69. Ray Bradbury, 1975

Ray Bradbury
Author, screenwriter

My connection to the noted sci-fi writer came through Man'ha Garreau-Dombasle, a retired French diplomat. She had saved the young Bradbury's life years earlier in Mexico at a *Día de los Muertos* celebration when he had fallen deathly ill. "Take my car," she said. "The driver will find you medical assistance." He had never forgotten her kindness, and they had remained friends. I visited her often in France, and once when I was going to Los Angeles she suggested I contact him with her greetings. She thought he would be interested in my newly created Apollo Muses Center for the Arts in New Jersey. I sent Bradbury a note, and received in response a large, colorfully decorated envelope filled with selected press clippings and two of his short plays. He cordially invited me to make use of these plays at Apollo Muses events.

70. *Madeleine Albright, circa 1997*

Madeleine Albright
Diplomat, Secretary of State

"I am not a Wellesley graduate," I confessed to Madeleine Albright as she took my hand at the end of a receiving line of well-wishing Wellesley women. It was at a Wellesley alumnae lecture she had given at the University of London. I had situated myself at the end of the line in the hopes that we might have an opportunity to converse beyond just a thank-you formality. To my delight, she kept a firm grip on my hand throughout our conversation. Albright exuded warmth and intelligence that I found endearing. This memorable day had begun and ended in London, with a visit to Cambridge for lunch at Corpus Christi College in between (at the high table, no less!) Then a rare Vermeer exhibition at the Fitzwilliam Museum just down the cobblestone street, and back to London for the Albright talk. What a day!

71. Leontyne Price, 1994

LEONTYNE PRICE
Operatic soprano

"These designs are very different from those done for me," the pioneering African-American soprano said, glancing over at some José Varona sketches for opera costumes. She was referring to Franco Zefferelli's infamous designs for his production of *Antony and Cleopatra,* which had opened the new Metropolitan Opera House at Lincoln Center in 1966 with Leontyne Price in the lead. It had been a fraught premiere, with set and lighting malfunctions, awkward costumes, an orchestra labor dispute (resolved just before the third act curtain), and Miss Price at one point finding herself trapped beneath a pyramid. The current occasion was the opening night reception for my design exhibition at the Capricorn Gallery. To my surprise, no one else seemed to have noticed this statuesque woman of international repute in attendance. I regretted that there was not a photographer available to record our meeting. And I did not have time to tell her that I'd been there at that historic night in 1966 when she'd had to battle all that malfunctioning equipment. Despite the difficulties, she had generated vast excitement and risen above it all.

72. Ethel Merman, 1956

Ethel Merman
Musical star

"Where's Miles?" The unmistakable voice of Ethel Merman rang out from the back of the room at the opening night reception for the costume design exhibition at my gallery. Heads swiveled, and there she was, the inimitable Merm. Perfectly turned out in a demure white suit, she had gone unnoticed until she opened that famous mouth. Tony-winning designer Miles White had created many of her favorite costumes through the years, along with wonderful designs for countless Broadway musicals over a quarter of a century.

73. Princess Margaret and
Antony Armstrong-Jones, aka Lord Snowdon, 1960

Princess Margaret
Sister of Queen Elizabeth II

Antony Armstrong-Jones, aka Lord Snowdon
Photographer, husband of Princess Margaret

The strains of "God Save the Queen" filled the reception hall. Princess Margaret, representing her sister, stood less than ten feet away, facing me. On her right, her husband Tony Armstrong-Jones, aka Lord Snowdon, gazed at me warmly. It was clear both to me and to Princess Margaret that he was flirting with me. The bouquet of yellow roses she held began to tremble. I was not certain if Her Royal Highness was about to swat her husband or me with them. Though his boldness was astonishing, and in poor taste, I was flattered by his attentions. I executed a strategic retreat.

This was a curious evening, indeed. Alice Fordyce, whom I was escorting, suggested that we go to the Royal Ballet and attend the reception for Princess Margaret, but pass up the dinner following. Instead, we would go dancing at the Plaza Hotel where our favorite bandleader was playing. We would miss the pre-dance dinner, but we'd have plenty of fun. This amounted to foregoing two dinners, which had both been paid for, but we would get to enjoy the ballet and the dancing. It was an excellent, if expensive, way to stay trim.

74. Eric Gustafson with Kitty Carlisle Hart

KITTY CARLISLE HART
Actress, singer, TV personality

Kitty Carlisle Hart, who was married to the famous Broadway playwright and director Moss Hart, enjoyed a long career in film, theater, and television. She won enduring fame as the opera singer in the Marx Brothers' classic comedy *A Night at the Opera*, and appeared as a panelist for many years on TV's popular game show *To Tell the Truth*. We met on many occasions, and once shared a program for seniors in Morristown, NJ. I provided the chamber music concert through my Apollo Muses Center for the Arts, and Kitty gave a very amusing talk based on her career. Although at this point she was well on toward 90, she maintained a lively energy as she reminisced about her life in the theater. Years earlier, I had met her after a summer stock performance on Cape Cod. She had greeted me warmly in her dressing room. I was aware that she had something going with her young leading man, but she did not know that I did, as well!

75. Cliff Robertson in a publicity photograph for PT-109 (1963)

76. Dina Merrill, 1968

Cliff Robertson
Actor

Dina Merrill
Actress

Not long after his 1963 breakthrough success playing JFK in the film *PT 109*, Cliff Robertson asked me to show him and his fiancée Dina Merrill around the World's Fair at Flushing Meadows. Dina was the beautiful actress daughter of Marjorie Merriweather Post (for whom Mar-a-Lago was built), and the two made a particularly attractive couple to spend time with. Though I had not been to the sprawling Fair myself, I improvised, and we spent several enjoyable hours together. Cliff was fascinated to hear about the Opera costume party that David the First and I had given in New York. He suggested that I put on something like that for him in Los Angeles. It was too complicated for me to attempt, especially as success depended on my knowing the participants. Tempting, but no thanks.

77. Rock Hudson, 1954

ROCK HUDSON
Actor

When in doubt, don't! I thought as I walked with determination toward the bank of elevators at Rome's Grand Hotel. I had read that morning in the *Rome Daily American* that Rock was staying at the hotel while making a movie. I found out his room number, and slipped a note under his door suggesting that we might get together, As I was walking away I heard his door open, and turned to see the gorgeous actor standing there reading my note. I turned briefly and gave a regretful farewell wave to Rock Hudson, as he gazed at me with confusion. I left the hotel and mingled with the busy throng in the warm Roman night. *What if,* I wondered. I have been wondering ever since.

78. *Libby Holman, 1935*

LIBBY HOLMAN
Actress, singer, socialite, activist

It was a party at our Amagansett house, and my partner David the First had invited his new *affaire de coeur*. I tried to ignore it, but I was crushed.

"I don't know what's troubling you, but it will be all right," the woman on my right assured me, stroking my arm. She was the legendary torch singer Libby Holman. I barely knew her, but she was a great comfort to me that night, in contrast to my friends at the party who scarcely noticed my distress. Libby remarked on the Cartier lighter I had lain on the table. It was identical to one she had given to her great friend Montgomery Clift. I mentioned having seen him isolated in his glass house at the Pines. Libby and I seemed to connect, and our friendship grew after this Amagansett evening. We met up again by accident at the Venice Biennale, and then in New York. I adored being in her company. She died not long after our last meeting, an apparent suicide by carbon monoxide poisoning, in 1971.

79. Van Johnson, 1947

VAN JOHNSON
Actor

The last thing I expected at a swanky JFK election day cocktail party on the East Side of Manhattan was a very emphatic goose! This surprise was heightened when I realized it was delivered by Van Johnson, that nice boy-next-door in those June Allyson feel-good movies during the war. My illusion that he must be straight was quickly corrected. I was too shy to come up with a clever retort, but Joan Fontaine, who was sitting on the floor leaning against the wall with drink in her hand, snickered. My face turned red. The party went on.

80. *Hermione Gingold, (undated, 1950s)*

Hermione Gingold
Actress

Van Johnson and several other actors, including the famous British comedienne Hermione Gingold, rented former maid's rooms on the top floor of a building on East 53rd Street. It made a convenient *pied-a-terre* for performers while in New York. Hermione told me she once knocked on Van's door to borrow a cup of money!

I met Hermione on an Atlantic crossing on the *Liberté*. She talked me into disembarking in England rather than going on to France as I had planned. I had made a point of including her in my crowd aboard ship, so I was offended when she turned to me on the platform at Victoria Station and, amidst the popping flashbulbs of the London press, blandly asked me, "What is your name?"

Hermione had invited me to escort her that evening to a formal event. I begged off, preferring to spend the night with my friend David Halliday who was starring on the West End in *West Side Story*. That was a very much more satisfactory way to enjoy my first night in London than with a silly actress who could not remember my name after my friendly attentions to her aboard ship.

ROBERT STACK
Actor

JANET LEIGH
Actress

Before going to dinner with my English friend Allegra Kent Taylor and her husband Douglas at a new restaurant in Los Angeles, we were invited by Robert Stack and his wife Rosemary to enjoy a pre-prandial drink at their lovely Brentwood home. Robert showed me the pool and tennis court. I said I'd love to play on his court. He seemed pleased at the the idea of my returning, though perhaps not necessarily for tennis. He mentioned that Janet Leigh played there frequently, so we would have to work out a time to play that didn't conflict with her schedule.

Later at the restaurant, I glanced across the room and with surprise noticed Janet Leigh there with two people. Those big eyes were fixed upon me. As dinner came to an end, Janet got rid of her dinner partners and sauntered sensuously over to our table. She wore a pantsuit and a simple gold chain that fell into her very ample cleavage. I introduced myself and mentioned we'd just been at the Stacks, and Robert had told me she played tennis there all the time.

"All the time?" she exclaimed, thrusting her breasts forward. "Oh, no. I spread myself all over town!"

It occurred to me that Stack might have called her while we were at his house to alert her that there was a new guy in town, and to tell her where we would be dining. They might have been playfully curious to see which of them would snare me.

81. *Janet Leigh and Robert Stack (collage)*

JEROME HINES
Operatic bass

FRANCO CORELLI
Operatic tenor

After the death of her husband, Olga Bloom bought an old coffee barge and literally built Bargemusic with her own hands. She wanted to create a space for young professional musicians to perform. (This was a founding principle I used to create Apollo Muses.) Olga moored the barge at the Brooklyn side of the Brooklyn Bridge, and refitted the interior into a concert space. She then set to work building a following of supporters. Many people responded to hearing classical music beautifully played in this attractive setting, with Manhattan across the river as a backdrop. Olga was beloved for her warmth, and infectious enthusiasm by audiences and musicians alike.

Apollo Muses rented this enchanting space for annual fund raisers. I presented the Apollo's Lyre Award with a concert and black-tie dinner aboard Bargemusic celebrating an outstanding personality in the arts for endeavors to help young artists. One of our most memorable events there honored Jerome Hines, the veteran Metropolitan Opera bass who created OMTI (Opera Music Theater International) to showcase young singers. Famed tenor Franco Corelli was on hand to present the award. Jerome's wife Lucia Evangelista translated Corelli's Italian. It was very amusing as the two singers sparred regularly in their appearances together during their careers.

Franco was one of the handsomest tenors in the opera world, and was always a favorite of Mr. Bing, General Manager of the Met. I had thrilled at Corelli's performances over the years, and was delighted to have involved him in this program. We also dined together a few times, with his wife always keeping a watchful eye.

82. Franco Corellli

83. Jerome Hines as Boris Godunov. Photograph inscribed: "To my good friend and colleague, Eric — Jerry Hines"

84. Oliver Smith

Oliver Smith
Scenic designer, interior designer

"What a delightful invitation to join your Holiday gathering. Unfortunately, I have arranged to be away until after New Year's," I replied with regret to Oliver Smith. I would have relished visiting this famous scenic designer's beautiful Brooklyn Heights townhouse, where Jackie Kennedy sometimes came to get drawing lessons from him.

85. Cecil Beaton, arriving at Eton (circa 1930s)

CECIL BEATON
Photographer, designer, diarist

The sting of having to turn down Oliver Smith's holiday party invitation was all the keener because Oliver had told me that Cecil Beaton would be among the guests, and he felt Cecil would enjoy meeting me. However, sometime later Cecil signed a couple of his books for me, in a more personal atmosphere.

86. Anne Jackson, 1968

87. Eli Wallach, in a publicity photograph for The Good, the Bad, and the Ugly (1966)

Anne Jackson
Actress

Eli Wallach
Actor

A reading of Elizabeth Bishop's poetry was on the program of Apollo Muses Center for the Arts during one summer's season at the Lu Shan Farm. Anne Jackson, who with her husband Eli Wallach made up one of the theater's royal couples, agreed to come for a couple of days and do the Sunday reading. It was a great coup for me and the program. Eli lent me their car to transport this remarkable actress to New Jersey and back. I had long admired her career and was thrilled to spend time with her. Back at their East Hampton home, a seafood dinner with her husband climaxed an eventful weekend.

Clare Boothe Luce
Writer, diplomat

"There are two things that I never had in my life," Clare Boothe Luce would announce to astonished dinner guests. This was a woman who was infamous for getting what she wanted. Her thirst for fame began early when living with her mother (of questionable repute) in a shabby apartment over a pet store on Sixth Avenue in Manhattan. Clare put her lovely complexion, beautiful blue eyes, and clever mind to work, starting in a lowly position at Condé Nast. Her climb up the social ladder culminated in her seducing Henry R. Luce, founder of *Time* magazine.

Lila, Luce's wife and the mother of their two young boys, was deeply hurt when he asked for a divorce to marry Clare. Lila promised her mother that she would never invite Clare to Lu Shan, the magnificent French chateau that Henry built for the family in New Jersey. Henry never spent a night there, and Clare never received an invitation.

I, however, enjoyed Lila's friendship and hospitality for some twenty-five years as her *"petit frère."* Over the years, Clare was aware of our friendship, as Lila and I entertained frequently and travelled the world together. Lila must have spoken affectionately about Eric (me!) at family gatherings where Clare was present. Also, their mutual friends and acquaintances must have made references which stirred Clare's curiosity. After each dinner where Clare mentioned her regret at the two things missing from her life, my phone would ring.

"You will never guess who I had dinner with last night. Clare Boothe Luce! Guess what she regrets not ever having had? A visit to Lu Shan, and Eric in her life!" It was amazing to contemplate this notoriously famous woman who took what she wanted, obsessing over these two things missing from her life. One of them was me!

88. *Clare Boothe Luce, 1944*

Epilogue

The stars have done their work, as have I, though I have worn many different hats to varying success. Aside from my more traditional accomplishments in the various arts, it is the FIRSTS that I relish the most:

1. While at Parke-Bernet Galleries, I came up with the idea of using the telephone for an entire sale with one client, long distance. It was standard practice to have a client on the phone from the auction podium for some minutes during the sale of a particular item. I used the public phone at the rear of the gallery for a lengthy call to New Orleans, making bids from there for the entire sale. After almost three hours, I secured a few paintings for my elated customer, making history in the process. *Art News* wrote the event up in 1963.

2. Shortly thereafter, I pointed out to management that the auction room, which was dark on most evenings, was a perfect location for an occasional concert or lecture. Many people were too intimidated to enter Parke-Bernet, but a $10 ticket to an evening concert or lecture would give them the confidence to investigate the hallowed display rooms and auction room in comfort. This, I suggested, would lead to more active participation during regular hours. It was a success.

3. Calling her "a woman Sunday painter," the New Mexico Museum of Art in Santa Fe rejected Georgia O'Keeffe's mural proposal. She never forgave the Santa Fe art community. When I took over the directorship of the Capricorn Gallery in New York in 1969, women artists were still held in lower esteem than their male counterparts. I disagreed and showcased several fine women artists. They and the public responded warmly.

4. I considered original costume and scenic designs for opera, theater, and ballet to be the last of the Collectibles. By mounting international shows, I created a stable market for them and helped form both private and museum collections.

5. My creation of Apollo Muses Center for the Arts on the famed LuShan Farm in Chester, New Jersey ran in the black for almost 25 years. Summer Sundays offered visitors a full day of music, art, and performances in a beautiful natural setting for a modest fee. Intimacy with the performers and nature was assured by limiting admissions to not more than 40 people. A free *al fresco* lunch assured that all cars were parked before the concert began. New Yorkers found their way to Apollo Muses, as well as others from distant places.

International travel was always part of my schedule, with writing articles on travel and musical events when time and inclination permitted. After closing Apollo Muses Center for the Arts, I lectured internationally, and continued to write books.

Now that I have turned 90 years of age, I muse over my decades of energetic activity, and know it is time to put the pen down and take a nap.

Photographic Credits

Grateful acknowledgment is made for the use of these photographs. The following abbreviations are used to indicate Creative Commons licensing:

CC BY 2.0
>Attribution 2.0 Generic
>https://creativecommons.org/licenses/by/2.0/deed.en

CC BY-NC-SA 2.0
>Attribution-NonCommercial-ShareAlike 2.0 Generic

CC BY-SA 3.0
>Attribution-ShareAlike 3.0 Unported
>https://creativecommons.org/licenses/by-sa/3.0/deed.en

CC BY 4.0
>Attribution 4.0 International
>https://creativecommons.org/licenses/by/4.0/

CC BY-SA 4.0
>Attribution-ShareAlike 4.0 International
>https://creativecommons.org/licenses/by-sa/4.0/deed.en

1. Peter O'Toole in a still as the title character of *Lawrence of Arabia* (Horizon Pictures / Columbia Pictures, 1962).
2. Judy Garland in a 1945 publicity still from *The Harvey Girls* (Metro-Goldwyn Mayer, 1946), Eric Carpenter for Metro-Goldwyn Mayer. Wikimedia Commons: https://commons.wikimedia.org/wiki/File:Judy_Garland_The_Harvey_Girls_MGM_Publicity_still.jpeg.
3. "Joan Crawford" by Yousuf Karsh, 1948. Art Institute of Chicago: https://www.artic.edu/artworks/186984/joan-crawford. Fair use.
4. Promotional photograph of Christina Crawford, unknown photographer, 1950s or 1960s. Wikimedia Commons: https://

commons.wikimedia.org/wiki/File:Christina_Crawford_Publicity_Still_50s_or_60s.jpg.
5. Promotional photograph of Aaron Copland, CBS Television, 7 September 1962. Wikimedia Commons: https://commons.wikimedia.org/wiki/File:Aaron_Copland_in_1962.jpg.
6. "Photo of vocalist Rise Stevens," by Bender, NY, 6 April 1959. Wikimedia Commons: https://commons.wikimedia.org/wiki/File:Rise_Stevens_1959.jpg.
7. Snapshot of Christine Jorgensen with the author, at the Scandinavian Societies of New York Woman of the Year Award Ceremony, 7 March 1953. Unknown photographer. From the private collection of Eric Gustafson.
8. "Josephine Baker" by Lucien Waléry, circa 1927. Wikimedia Commons: https://commons.wikimedia.org/wiki/File:Josephine_Baker_5.jpg.
9. "James Dean, 1955," publicity photograph, unknown photographer, Film Star Vintage: https://www.flickr.com/photos/classicvintage/9194759559/. CC BY 2.0.
10. [Portrait of Georgia O'Keeffe, Abiquiu, N.M.] by Carl Van Vechten, 16 August 1950. Library of Congress, Prints & Photographs Division, Carl Van Vechten Collection, lot 12735, no. 892: https://lccn.loc.gov/2004663416.
11. Left to right: Celeste Holm, Eric Gustafson, and Ruth Warrick, in an undated snapshot, unknown photographer. From the private collection of Eric Gustafson.
12. Eric Gustafson in a personal snapshot with Celeste Holm, undated, unknown photographer. From the private collection Eric Gustafson.
13. Salvador Dalí and his wife Gala with friends, including, far right, Ysabel Aya, Eric Gustafson's "Colombian soul mate," unknown photographer. From the private collection of Eric Gustafson.
14. Lotte Lenya in a promotional photograph for *Die Dreigroschenoper / The Threepenny Opera* (Nero-Film / Tonbild-Syndikat AG (Tobis) / Warner Bros. Pictures GmbH, 1931).

15. Rudolf Nureyev in an undated snapshot. From the private collection of Eric Gustafson.
16. Photo of vocalist Risë Stevens. Bender, NY, 6 April 1959. Wikimedia Commons: https://commons.wikimedia.org/wiki/File:Rise_Stevens_1959.jpg.
17. Publicity photo, [American actress Rita Hayworth] by Whitey Schafer, 1942. Ænigma Images: https://www.aenigma-images.com/2017/04/a-l-whitey-schafer/.
18. Publicity portrait photo of Groucho Marx for *You Bet Your Life*, 1947. Wikimedia Commons: https://commons.wikimedia.org/wiki/File:Groucho_Marx_-_portrait.jpg.
19. Publicity photo of Veronica Lake for *I Wanted Wings*, 1941, Wikimedia Commons: https://commons.wikimedia.org/wiki/File:Veronica_Lake_-_Studio_portrait_(1941).png.
20. [Tallulah Bankhead while filming an episode of "Batman."]. Alabama Department of Archives and History, Tallulah Bankead Papers, http://archives-alabama-primo.hosted.exlibrisgroup.com/01ALABAMA:default_scope:01ALABAMA_ALMA215501010002743.
21. "Silver Pitcher presented to White House. Mrs. Kennedy. White House, Diplomatic Reception Room," by Abbie Rowe, 5 December 1961. John F. Kennedy Library, National Archives and Records Administration: https://catalog.archives.gov/id/194176.
22. Eric Gustafson in a personal snapshot with Bess and Harry S Truman, 1960 or 1961. Unknown photographer. From the private collection of Eric Gustafson.
23. Extract from "Photograph of Secretary of State Henry Kissinger and Lee Bouvier Radziwill, Sister of Jacqueline Kennedy Onassis, at a State dinner Honoring Chancellor Bruno Kreisky of Austria," unknown photographer, 12 November 1974. Gerald R. Ford Presidential Library, National Archives and Records Administration: https://catalog.archives.gov/id/7462064.

24. [Doris Duke], unknown photographer, scanned from the 1951 edition of *The Chanticleer*, the yearbook of Duke University. Wikimedia Commons: https://commons.wikimedia.org/wiki/File:Doris_Duke_1951_(cropped).jpg.
25. Snapshot of Grace Bumbry and Eric Gustafson, unknown photographer, undated. **From the private collection of Eric Gustafson.**
26. Eric Gustafson (left) with Sir Harold Acton in the formal palace gardens of La Pietra outside Florence, unknown photographer, undated. **From the private collection of Eric Gustafson.**
27. "Helen, Queen Mother of Romania," National Portrait Gallery (UK): https://www.npg.org.uk/collections/search/portrait/mw71267/Helen-Queen-Mother-of-Romania. Used by permission of the National Potrait Gallery.
28. Dame Joan Sutherland in an undated publicity photograph, inscribed "For Eric — Best Wishes, Joan Sutherland." From the private collection Eric Gustafson.
29. Beverly Sills in an undated publicity photograph, inscribed "To Eric — For his Hall of Fame — Love, Beverly Sills." From the private collection Eric Gustafson.
30. Publicity photograph of Joan Sutherland and Beverly Sills, in a rare appearance together, San Diego, 1980. Photograph inscribed to Eric Gustafson. From the private collection of Eric Gustafson.
31. "Andy Warhol with Archie, his pet Dachshund," by Jack Mitchell, 1973. Wikimedia Commons: https://commons.wikimedia.org/wiki/File:Andy_Warhol_by_Jack_Mitchell.jpg. **CC BY 4.0.**
32. Alvin Ailey in an undated publicity photograph, inscribed "*For Eric — Because he is who he is — and quite quite divinely crazy!*" dated 13 February 1975. From the private collection Eric Gustafson.
33. Greta Garbo in a still by an unknown photographer from *Anna Christie* (Metro-Goldwyn Mayer, 1930).

34. Snapshot of **Anthony Perkins and Mia Farrow,** unknown photographer, undated. **From the private collection of Eric Gustafson.**
35. Edward Mulhare in a publicity still for *The Ghost and Mrs. Muir* (Twentieth Century Fox Television / ABC). Michael Ochs Archives / Getty Images.
36. [Operatic mezzo-soprano Jennie Tourel, New York], by Roman Vishniac, circa 1943. International Center of Photography, Accession No. 2012.80.52: https://www.icp.org/browse/archive/objects/operatic-mezzo-soprano-jennie-tourel-new-york-0.
37. Leonard Bernstein in an undated promotional photograph by an unknown photographer. **From the private collection Eric Gustafson.**
38. [Gertrude Stein and Virgil Thomson looking at a musical score.] https://dp.la/item/120bf95d35fc6cdc0bc9de66b56f461d. Thérèse Bonney, © The Regents of the University of California, The Bancroft Library, University of California, Berkeley. CC BY 4.0.
39. Publicity photo of **Zsa Zsa Gabor,** 1959, Rogers & Cowan. Wikimedia Commons: https://commons.wikimedia.org/wiki/File:Zsa_Zsa_Gabor_-_1959.jpg.
40. [Robert Indiana] by Dennis Griggs. Wikimedia Commons: https://commons.wikimedia.org/wiki/File:Robert_Indiana.jpg. CC BY-SA 4.0.
41. Dennis Hopper, unknown photographer, from *News and Events*, Rochester Institute of Technology (RIT), 6 April 1973. Wikimedia Commons: https://commons.wikimedia.org/wiki/File:Dennis_Hopper,_RIT_NandE_1973_Apr6_Complete.jpg.
42. Frederica von Stade, in an undated publicity photograph, along with a letter to Eric Gustafson dated March 27, 1998. **From the private collection of Eric Gustafson.**
43. [Portrait of Gloria Vanderbilt and Wyatt Cooper] by Carl Van Vechten, 18 February 1964. Library of Congress, Prints & Photographs Division, Carl Van Vechten Collection, lot 12735, no. 1134: https://www.loc.gov/pictures/resource/van.5a52733/.

44. [Portrait of Samuel Barber] by Carl Van Vechten, 11 December 1944. Library of Congress, Prints & Photographs Division, Carl Van Vechten Collection, lot 12735, no. 98: https://www.loc.gov/pictures/resource/van.5a51697/.
45. Snapshot of Gian Carlo Menotti (right) with Willem de Kooning, along with an accompanying note to Ysabel Aya, unknown photographer, undated. From the private collection of Eric Gustafson.
46. Gustav III in coronation robes, cropped from "Gustav III (1746–1792), kung av Sverige, 1777" by Alexander Roslin. Nationalmuseum: Sveriges konst och designmuseum (National Museum: Sweden's Art and Design Museum), artwork ID 155330, https://collection.nationalmuseum.se/sv/collection/item/15330/; Wikimedia Commons: https://commons.wikimedia.org/wiki/File:Gustav_III_(1746-1792),_King_of_Sweden,_in_coronation-robes_(Alexander_Roslin)_-_Nationalmuseum_-_15330_(cropped).tif
47. [Queen Sylvia at the celebration of the centenary of Stockholm's City Hall] by Frankie Fouganthin, 22 June 2023. Wikimedia Commons: https://commons.wikimedia.org/wiki/File:Queen_Silvia_of_Sweden_in_June_2023-2_(cropped).jpg. CC BY-SA 4.0.
48. "Willem de Kooning in his studio," by Antony di Gesu, 1961. Wikimedia Commons: https://commons.wikimedia.org/wiki/File:Willem_de_Kooning_in_his_studio.jpg, citing Smithsonian Institution Archives. Local Number SIA2011-2241.
49. "Photograph of Gayelord Hauser in 1961," Wikimedia Commons: https://commons.wikimedia.org/wiki/File:Gayelord_Hauser_1961.png, citing Gayelord Hauser, *Mirror, Mirror On the Wall: Invitation to Beauty* (New York: Farrar, Straus and Cudahy, 1961).
50. Snapshot of Elizabeth Taylor and Eric Gustafson, unknown photographer, undated. From the private collection of Eric Gustafson.

51. Snapshot of Elizabeth Taylor and R. C. Gorman, unknown photographer, undated. From the private collection of Eric Gustafson.
52. "Betty Ford," unknown photographer, 1980. Wikimedia Commons: https://commons.wikimedia.org/wiki/File:BETTYFORD.jpg, citing Betty Ford Center and Gerald Ford Presidential Museum, National Archives and Records Administraion, Image 2008-NLF-019 : https://www.fordlibrarymuseum.gov/galleries/media-photo-kit-first-lady-betty-ford#3681. Image courtesy of Betty Ford Center.
53. Snapshot of Catherine Deneuve, at the Sherry-Netherland dinner-dance with Eric Gustafson, unknown photographer, undated. From the private collection of Eric Gustafson.
54. Snapshot of Holly Woodlawn by Eric Gustafson. Eric, Accompanied by a note: "Thank you for that fabulous photo, Love you, Holly." From the private collection of Eric Gustafson.
55. "Andrew Robert the 11th Duke of Devonshire outside Chatsworth," by Allan Warren, undated. Wikimedia Commons: https://en.wikipedia.org/wiki/File:Andrew_Robert_11th_Duke_of_Devonshire.jpg. CC BY-SA 3.0 .
56. Pope John XXIII in an undated photograph, released by the Holy See in 2010. Catholic News Service, The Vatican.
57. Lillian Gish in a still from *Way Down East* (D. W. Griffith Productions, 1920).
58. Publicity photograph of Greer Garson, unknown photographer, undated (1940s), Metro-Goldwyn Mayer.
59. [James Baldwin taken in Hyde Park London] by Allan Warren. Wikimedia Commons: https://commons.wikimedia.org/wiki/File:James_Baldwin_33_Allan_Warren.jpg. CC BY-SA 3.0.
60. Leslie Caron from the cover of *Eiga no Tomo* (December 1953). Wikimedia Commons: https://commons.wikimedia.org/wiki/File:Eiganotomo-lesliecaron-dec1953.jpg.
61. Jean-Louis Barrault in a still from *Les Enfants du Paradis* (Société Nouvelle Pathé Cinéma, 1945).

A Path Lit by Stars

62. Jane Goodall by Johanna Lohr, *Steingarts Morning Briefing*, 2019. CC BY-SA 4.0.
63. Snapshot of Alexandra "Choura" Danilova with Eric Gustafson, unknown photographer, circa 1962. From the private collection Eric Gustafson.
64. Snapshot of **Tennessee Williams** by Eric Gustafson. From the private collection Eric Gustafson.
65. Mae West in an undated publicity photograph, inscribed "To Eric Sin-cerely." From the private collection Eric Gustafson.
66. Snapshot of William Hurt by Eric Gustafson. From the private collection Eric Gustafson.
67. Truman Capote and Martha Mitchell, in a still from The Pat Collins Show (CBS Television, 7 May 1975), posted as truman-capote-martha-mitchell-500 (https://www.flickr.com/photos/trumancapote/17183865647/) by Peggy O'Connor (https://www.flickr.com/people/trumancapote/). CC BY-NC-SA 2.0.
68. [Portrait of playwright Edward Albee] by the *Los Angeles Times*, 16 May 1975. Wikimedia Commons: https://commons.wikimedia.org/wiki/File:Edward_Albee,_1975.jpg; citing the *Los Angeles Times* Photographic Collection at the UCLA Library: https://digital.library.ucla.edu/catalog/ark:/21198/zz0002pxjf. CC BY 4.0.
69. Ray Bradbury by Alan Light, August 1975. Wikimedia Commons: https://commons.wikimedia.org/wiki/File:Ray_Bradbury_(1975).jpg. Photo by Alan Light. CC BY 2.0.
70. Madeleine Albright, official secretary of State portrait, circa 1997. Wikimedia Commons: https://commons.wikimedia.org/wiki/File:Madeleine_Albright_1997.jpg; citing the Office of the Historian of the United States Department of State: https://history.state.gov/departmenthistory/people/albright-madeleine-korbel.
71. "Leontyne Price" by Jack Mitchell, 1994. Wikimedia Commons: https://commons.wikimedia.org/wiki/File:Leontyne_Price_(color)_by_Jack_Mitchell_cropped.jpg. CC BY-SA 4.0.

72. Promotional photograph of Ethel Merman in the Broadway musical, *Happy Hunting*, Cris Alexander, 27 July 1956. Wikimedia Commons: https://commons.wikimedia.org/wiki/File:Ethel_Merman_1956.JPG.
73. Princess Margaret and Anthony Armstrong-Jones spending the weekend at the Royal Lodge. 1960. Pleasure Photo: https://pleasurephoto.wordpress.com/2017/01/15/lord-snowdon-with-princess-margaret-1960/.
74. Snapshot of Kitty Carlisle Hart with Eric, unknown photographer, undated. From the private collection Eric Gustafson.
75. Publicity photograph of Cliff Robertson in *PT109* (Warner Brothers, 1963). Internet Movie Database: https://www.imdb.com/title/tt0057393/mediaviewer/rm940011777/.
76. Publicity photograph of Dina Merrill by John Engstead, Helen Ferguson Public Relations-Los Angeles, 1968. Wikimedia Commons: https://commons.wikimedia.org/wiki/File:Dina_Merrill_1968.JPG.
77. Rock Hudson in an uncredited Universal Pictures photograph published in *Modern Screen* magazine, 1954. Wikimedia Commons: https://commons.wikimedia.org/wiki/File:Rock_Hudson_bw_1954.jpg; citing *Modern Screen*, September 1954, p. 42.
78. Libby Holman by Maurice Seymour, undated (1930–1950). Wikimedia Commons: https://commons.wikimedia.org/wiki/File:Libby_holman_seymour.jpg.
79. Van Johnson by Eric Carpenter, June 1947. Wikimedia Commons: https://commons.wikimedia.org/wiki/File:Van_Johnson_by_Eric_Carpenter,_1947.jpg.
80. Hermione Gingold in the 1950s, by Esudiotin. Wikimedia Commons: https://commons.wikimedia.org/wiki/File:Hermione_Gingold_in_the_1950s_(cropped).jpg. CC BY-SA 3.0.
81. Robert Stack and Janet Leigh in a collage by Julian Hands. From the private collection of Eric Gustafson.

82. Franco Corelli in a promotional photograph by an unknown photographer. Princeton University, WPRB, Sandy's Opera Gallery: https://www.cs.princeton.edu/~san/corelli5.jpg.
83. Jerome Hines, as Boris Godunov in a promotional photograph, unknown photographer, undated. Inscribed: "To my good friend and colleague, Eric — Jerry Hines." From the private collection of Eric Gustafson.
84. OliverSmith, unknown photographer, undated. Find a Grave, database and images (https://www.findagrave.com/memorial/235113127/oliver_lemuel-smith: accessed December 7, 2025), memorial page for Oliver Lemuel Smith (13 Feb 1918–23 Jan 1994), Find a Grave Memorial ID 235113127; Maintained by Andrew Masullo (contributor 48550567).
85. Cecil Beaton arriving at Eton, unknown photographer, 1930s. Wikimedia Commons: https://commons.wikimedia.org/wiki/File:Cecil_Beaton_arriving_at_an_Eton_restored.JPG.
86. Anne Jackson in *The Secret Life of an American Wife* (20th Century Fox, 1968). Wikimedia Commons: https://commons.wikimedia.org/wiki/File:Anne_Jackson_1968.jpg.
87. Publicity photo of Eli Wallach for the film *The Good, the Bad and the Ugly* (United Artists, 1966). Wikimedia Commons: https://commons.wikimedia.org/wiki/File:Eli_Wallach_-_publicity.jpg.
88. Clare Boothe Luce accepting applause after delivering her "G. I. Jim" keynote speech at the Republican National Convention, Chicago, Illinois, June 27, 1944. "G.O.P Luminary," Acme Newspictures, Inc. Collection of the U.S. House of Representatives, accession number: PA2016.01.0084c: https://history.house.gov/Collection/Detail/15032445089.

About the Author

R. Eric Gustafson's life has unfolded like one of the richly layered stage sets he has spent a lifetime studying — full of shifting lights, hidden passages, and the unexpected entrances of remarkable characters. Born in the Bronx in 1935, Gustafson came of age in a New York brimming with artistic possibility. After earning a B.A. from Queens College and an M.F.A. in theater from Carnegie Mellon University, he stepped directly into the world he had long admired, joining Parke-Bernet Galleries as a young consultant. There he served an extraordinary clientele — Greta Garbo, Elizabeth Taylor, Jacqueline Kennedy — absorbing both the elegance and the eccentricities of the cultural elite while sharpening the discriminating eye that would define his curatorial work.

During the 1960s and '70s, Gustafson became a spirited ambassador for theater design, organizing exhibitions that traced the art form's lineage and teased out its contemporary vitality. From Spoleto to Santa Fe to the great museums of New York, he curated more than a dozen influential shows, including "A Tribute to the Old Met," "The Stage Is Set," and the much-admired "Designs for a Prima Donna: Dame Joan Sutherland." His early embrace of contemporary art at Santa Fe's Jamison Galleries revealed his instinct for creative risk and his fondness for artists whose imaginations exceeded the boundaries of genre.

His scholarship and curatorial grace led naturally to the podium. Over several decades, Gustafson lectured at the Cooper-Hewitt Museum, the Library for the Performing Arts at Lincoln Center, Vizcaya (Miami), universities across the U.S., and art institutions in London, Paris, and Spoleto, Italy. Museums sought his guidance;

he advised collections at Cooper-Hewitt, the Museum of the City of New York, the Harvard Theater Collection, and the Tobin Collection, helping shape the historical record of theater design.

Yet perhaps his most generous contribution came through the Apollo Muses Center for the Arts, the New Jersey organization he founded in 1983 and led for more than twenty years. On the grounds of Lu Shan Farm — his longtime friend Lila Hotz Luce Tyng's evocative estate — he produced more than 230 classical music concerts and a similar number of programs in theater, dance, and visual art. These were sunny Sunday afternoons where celebrated artists such as Celeste Holm, Franco Corelli, and Toshiko Takaezu shared the stage with emerging talents, the well-known and the unknown held in equal regard. Gustafson's belief in the promise of young artists became one of his signature themes.

As a writer, he has moved fluidly between memoir, travel narrative, and cultural history. *The Court Theaters of Europe* (1982) explored the theatrical past with the intimacy of a confidant. His previous memoirs — *Cinderella Is a Man: A Picaresque Passage to Serenity*, *Last Guy Waltzing: A Tale of Reinvention*, and *A Kaleidoscope: Fragments of Memory* — trace his own reinventions with candor and wry delight. India became a second home and a deep well of inspiration; his books *India: Paradox & Treasures* and *Expect the Unexpected* capture the country's inexhaustible surprises. In *My Beloved Southwest*, he gathered a lifetime of Santa Fe impressions.

After decades of orbiting Santa Fe for work and friendship, Gustafson settled there permanently in 2006. He continues to write, reflect, and welcome serendipity — the faithful companion of a life lived with curiosity, hospitality, and wonder.

Current Coyote Arts Titles

Gilbert Alter-Gilbert, editor. *Pipe Dreams: The Drug Experience in Literature*

Greg Boyd. *Brotherton's Travels: Memoirs*

Jefferson Carter. *Free Hugs: New and Selected Poems*

Eric Gustafson. *A Path Lit by Stars: Reminiscences*

Joe Martin. *Rumi's Mathnavi: A Theatre Adaptation*

Lawrence Millman. *Goodbye, Ice: Arctic Poems*

Lawrence Millman. *Outsider: My Boyhood with Thoreau* (illustrated by Geoff Halverson)

Elias Papadimitrakopoulos. *Toothpaste with Chlorophyll | Maritime Hot Baths* (translated from the Greek by John Taylor; illustrated by Alekos Fassianos)

Eric Paul Shaffer. *A Million-Dollar Bill: Poems*

Eric Paul Shaffer. *Free Speech: poem sequences*

Eric Paul Shaffer. *Green Leaves: Selected & New Poems*

Christopher Spranger. *The Book of Tasks, Volume I: Atlantean Undertakings*

Christopher Spranger. *The Comedy of Agony: A Book of Poisonous Contemplations*

Leslie Stahlhut. *The Secret of the Old Cloche: Agatha Christine Mystery Stories, #1*

John Taylor. *What Comes from the Night: Poems*

Forthcoming Coyote Arts Titles

Eric Basso. *Fictions: The Beak Doctor: Short Fictions, 1972–1976 & Bartholomew Fair*

René Daumal. *The Anti-Heaven* (translated and with an introduction by Jordan Jones)

Jordan Jones. *The Wheel: Poems*

Kendall Lappin. *Dead French Poets Speak Plain English & Memoirs of a Translator of Poetry*

Joe Martin. *Parabola: Shorter Fictions*

Gérard de Nerval. *Aurélia, followed by Sylvie* (translated by Kendall Lappin and with an introduction by Eric Basso)

Eric Paul Shaffer. *Second Nature: Poems*

Leslie Stahlhut. *Borderlands of the Heart and Other Stories*

Leslie Stahlhut. *The Hidden Staircase: Agatha Christine Mystery Stories, #2*

www.ingramcontent.com/pod-product-compliance
Lightning Source LLC
Chambersburg PA
CBHW030520080526
44586CB00011B/273